FIRST THINGS FIRST: Putting Students Before Standards

A Practical Guide for Building Positive and Engaged Learning Communities

Tawio J. Barksdale, Ed.D.

Text Copyright © 2021 by Tawio J. Barksdale

All rights reserved. No part of this book may be reproduced, scanned, or distributed in any printed or electronic form or by any means without prior written consent of the author, except for brief quotes used in reviews. Please do not participate in or encourage piracy of copyrighted materials in violation of the author's rights. Purchase only authorized editions.

Published by

Hadassah's Crown Publishing, LLC

Simpsonville, SC

ISBN 978-1-950894-58-1

Printed in the United States

Contents

Introduction   v

1. Understanding the Pedagogy of Stakeholder Engagement   5
2. Messages Matter   28
3. Confronting Bias   50
4. Confronting the Impact of White Privilege on Systems and Schooling   82
5. Taking Ownership for Being First Responders   101
6. We Cannot Have It Both Ways – Foundations for Creating Equitable Culture   109
7. Is Being an Educator the Right Profession for You or Is It Just the Right Thing to Do?   122

Acknowledgments   128

References   131

Introduction

For quite some time in education, an overabundance of student behavior, performance, and aptitude has been exclusively determined, measured, and stigmatized by state test scores, diagnostic test scores, letter grades on report cards, and disciplinary referrals. Organizational decisions about Individualized Education Programs (IEPs), academic placement, and decisions about suspensions or expulsions (to name a few) are based upon the educational community's heavy reliance on narrow scopes of student data deemed important by the bureaucracy – a system perpetuated by dominant culture norms informed by the power and privilege structures existing within the bureaucracies of our country's institutions.

Consequently, a high number of students remain marginalized and fall through the cracks year after year due to overreliance on bureaucratic policy which emphasizes the overuse of the same limited scope of data that overlooks students' individuality. This sends a clear message that meeting true student needs is not the priority. The misallocated use of this data contributes to stifling achievement because it provides an incomplete and misrepresented academic picture for so many students. Because the educational community has continuously relied on the same data relative to decision-making, it has compelled parents and society to do the same. Now, parents and society at large are more attentive to bureaucratic metrics, such as standardized test scores and the number of free and reduced lunch student populations in schools, than they are to the holistic capacity of schools' resources (i.e. quality of student programs, staff involvement, school climate, etc.). While frequency may vary, these and other dominant culture norms are the catalysts for why misconduct, mismanagement, and underachievement significantly impact districts and schools within our educational community.

Many districts and schools think they are doing everything right because they measure up to bureaucratic metrics of good test scores and good public report card results. However, these districts and schools are just as much at-risk for student underperformance if they become complicit with existing patterns where one student or group of students continuously fall through the cracks. Shifting the paradigm requires a change in the way we do business in many districts, schools, classrooms, and most importantly, in mindset. The fact is if the educational community chooses to make bureaucratic expectations, which are often premised around the norms of the White privilege and dominant culture perceptions of schooling, the priority districts and schools will continue using narrow scopes of data as well as cookie-cutter approaches that hinder possibilities of high achievement for many of our students. It also requires us as an educational community to spend more time and reflection on the "pedagogy of stakeholder engagement" to ensure that practices and approaches are more student centered rather than system centered. The pedagogy of stakeholder engagement is discussed in greater depth in Chapter 1. However, the more we actively and constructively engage the diverse contingency of stakeholders within our learning community, the better our chances are of meeting the needs of a broader group of students and subsequently, advancing levels of achievement for all instead of just a few groups of students.

My occupational history consists of having been a classroom teacher, an academic and athletic coach, a brief tenure in school administration, and a school as well as district behavior coach and interventionist. Additionally, I spent a few years in investment banking. The reason for sharing my experiences is not to impress you with my resume. Rather, it is to connect a central contextual theme to all of them; a theme which will be critical to be aware of as you navigate this book. Whether my job was in selling stocks and bonds or teaching standards, the common theme that was critical to being successful was having an ability to interact and be personable with essential stakeholders (students, parents, administrators, or clients). While I had minimal experience in sales when I began my career as a financial advisor, it was the pedagogy of stakeholder engagement that compelled individuals as well as groups of clients to trust a virtual novice with investing multi-million dollars of assets into what were often volatile markets.

What does all of that have to do with this book? Covering state standards and achieving high test scores are at the epicenter of what governs the educational expectations of states, districts, schools, and teachers when considering most educational decisions. While academic standards and testing in and of themselves are not a bad thing, their value is misrepresented when the message appears to be that covering standards and high achievement on tests are more important than meeting the holistic developmental needs of **ALL** the students we serve. If the focus is on meeting students' holistic needs, mastery of standards and higher achievement will be the subsequent byproduct. Therefore, the approach affording us the best chance of meeting student needs and ultimately improving their performance is placing more focus on the pedagogy of stakeholder engagement and interaction instead of on pedagogies specifying how to teach the standards and achieve higher test scores. Our attitudes, our values, and our messaging need to show our stakeholders (especially students and their families) that meeting their needs is first. This will go a long way in improving cultures within districts and schools as well as increasing the stakeholder support within the educational community.

Whether it be the area of behavior or academics, the dominant culture and White privilege perspectives of "standards first" fosters an environment where students who come from traditional homes and lifestyles have a more increased likelihood for high achievement than students who come from non-traditional homes and lifestyles. If advocates and stakeholders of education are serious about providing a quality education and high achievement for all students, it is time for us as an educational community to be more serious about this duty and reflect on our approaches relative to diagnosing, assessing, and ultimately advancing student achievement for ALL learners. It is also important that we are sensitive to our methods for interacting with and engaging students and their families because some of our approaches send messages which encourage disengagement as well as disenfranchisement. This day and time call for teaching and learning to be about more than standards, test scores, and the rules and policies governed by bureaucratic norms. The process of fostering authentic teaching and learning cultures begins and ends with **putting students' diverse individual needs first!**

When I refer to student needs, I'm not necessarily referring to their needs existing within the confines of mastering standards, boosting their standardized test scores, or based on their results on the various diagnostic tests administered within schools and districts throughout the country. I am referencing their basic needs, socioemotional needs, and their need to belong and feel cared for in a nurturing and engaging culture. This book was written for those within the educational community who seek to explore meaningful approaches in growing their pedagogy of stakeholder engagement so that ALL students – not just the consistent few - have a higher likelihood of improved achievement.

Notifications

I feel it necessary to inform you I am intentionally critical of educators and mainstream education in this book. At first glance, it may appear I am bashing or belittling educators and the field of education. Having served as an educator for over 20 years, I have been on the front lines of schools – within the classroom, instructional coaching, administration, and behavior intervention. So, from my perspective, it is important you understand there is no bigger advocate for education and for educators than me. However, reflection and adjustments are necessary for improvement. Thus, it is essential for us as an educational community to assess our day-to-day operations and our pedagogies because it is important we abandon practices as well as patterns of thinking which hinder groups of students from realizing their true achievement potential.

Additionally, it is necessary to inform you that this book will confront prominent issues that will call for rigorous and often uncomfortable discourse in hopes of activating meaningful and constructive change. Further, there will be several themes and ideas intentionally and continuously repeated throughout this book because of their importance in reframing the narrative for what should be considered best practice. Adding new curriculum, protocol, or policy will not change the progress of achievement for students with the greatest needs if we as an educational community are not willing to investigate and confront the ideologies most impactful to the foundation of the current educational principles. Inserting new curriculum standards or policy to an insecure foundation will yield the same result as building a house on an insecure foundation. It will create a magnitude of problems and ultimately the structure will not have the ability to stand. That is the unfortunate consequence for many students in districts and schools. Curriculum, policy, and protocol expectations continue to be implemented into cultures where there are fractured ideological foundations. If ideological foundations are never improved, these additions will only contribute to routine student underperformance and misunderstood student behaviors. Inserting something new will not necessarily make things better if what is being inserted does not contribute to fixing the actual problem. Therefore, if the educational community continues placing emphasis on superficial aspects of education intended to appease the bureaucracy while only giving minimal attention to the aspects which matter the most, it will perpetuate student underachievement and underperformance for too many students who have the potential to achieve and perform far greater than the grades reflected on their report cards or the scores reflected on their state tests. I challenge all educators to seek to change certain ineffective practices of the status quo. Furthermore, I am hopeful your passion for improving students will inspire you to interpret this content as well as the discourse through a lens of pursuing improvement so all students have an increased likelihood of success and achievement instead of through a lens of assigning blame and implication.

There are generally three categories of educators. An abundance of educators (administrators, teachers, assistants, custodians, coaches, support staff, etc.) engage and interact with students every day with the genuine intentions of making each of them better regardless of how many adjustments or accommodations need to be made. For that constituency of educators, I ask that you please use the contents of this book as a reflective growth tool to deepen your reflection as well as professional growth in reaching students.

Second, there is a constituency of educators who have succumbed to the pressures of bureaucratic expectation and overzealous perceptions. While they may have a love for children and educating them, they have been swallowed in the abyss of standards, protocol, and policy which has subsequently made them lose focus of the importance of balance. This constituency of educators has allowed pacing guides, diagnostic tests, as well as systemic and personal bias relative to the letter of the law mentality to significantly influence their opinions and their interactions with students – opinions and interactions which hinder their abilities to build meaningful relationships with these most essential stakeholders. To this constituency of educators, I respectfully ask you to use the contents of this book as a tool to rebalance yourselves and reflect as well as rediscover your original motivation for becoming an educator – which is hopefully to positively inspire and impact the lives of ALL students.

Third, as in all professions, there will be some educators who interact with this book and their minds cannot be influenced or changed about how they choose to teach, interact with, and interpret the success of students. This constituency will likely continue to only view student achievement and success through a lens of what the bureaucracy of the dominant culture holds true – primarily labeling district and school communities as successful when they exhibit good test scores, good behavior, and parents who proactively advocate school staff, programs, policy, and protocol. While districts and schools achieving the aforementioned items are worth celebrating, solely relying on these items as metrics to indicate the depth of student achievement will often be misleading. Educators who have this mindset will more than likely experience more challenges in reaching and moving those students who are outside of the norms of the bureaucratic parameters mentioned above.

Realistically, there are an abundance of districts and schools with underprivileged and marginalized students and parents where they are productively growing students academically and socioemotionally along with actively engaging their families in ways bureaucrats are often inattentive to. So, to only view student success through the lens of bureaucratic expectation alienates a significant number of students who will subsequently continue being marginalized and underserved. To this constituency of educators, I ask you to thoughtfully consider that high student achievement and success are still possible even if students are not making all A's and B's, if they experience an infraction of a rule or two, and even if their parents are not the most traditionally supportive and do not attend every school function. If you are unable or unwilling to seriously consider these possibilities, I also respectfully ask your consideration to pursue another profession because remaining grounded in the rigidities of bureaucratic norms will almost certainly generate similar results for many of the same students who continue to underachieve but are capable of so much more.

High student achievement and success can happen in districts and schools where there are adjusted or modified schedules to accommodate for unique student needs and where every student does not score 'exemplary' or achieve the state expectation relative to standardized testing. I challenge the educational community to not view all the other pathways to success as detrimental because they do not directly correspond with the metrics, perceptions, and expectations having been programmed into us by the bureaucracy. When traveling to a destination, there are usually multiple routes one can take to get there. While travelers may have varying opinions about which route is most efficient, the important thing is the travelers safely arrive at the destination. Thus, there are multiple routes for helping students to arrive at the destination of high achievement, healthy development, and success. Some of those routes will look different from the route determined to be important by mainstream education and the bureaucracy.

It is essential we as an educational community transition away from the bondage of the "standards first" approach and gravitate towards the "stakeholder engagement" (student first) approach so we can increase the likelihood of high achievement for ALL our students. Doing so requires us to reflectively look in the mirror and adjust strategies, policies, and procedures working against our capacity to create equity and build individual and collective efficacy for improving achievement in our students along with gaining meaningful support from their families. These modifications and adjustments are especially important for improving achievement in our "nonmainstream students" – a term I will define and discuss in Chapter 1. So, while it may seem I am being critical of educators as well as education, I am doing so in hopes of prompting more reflection and keeping the attention on us (educators) because the shift can only happen effectively if it begins with us.

We cannot expect to change student, family, or stakeholder mindsets if we do not show willingness to be reflective and modify our mindsets and approaches (where applicable) so we become catalysts for affecting the change we desire to see. If we take responsibility and ownership of reflecting, adjusting, and modeling things in our practice that need to change, we assume the leadership in creating cultures that will inspire other stakeholders to do the same. Changing the culture will go a long way in changing outcomes – changes that are urgently needed for many students to achieve their potential within our educational system.

Furthermore, while the ideas and assertions relative to the content of this book are grounded in meaningful research, it was not written with the intentions of championing my knowledge of the research process. This is not intended to be the type of book filled with APA citations and research-based jargon to overwhelm its readers all for the benefit of substantiating claims. Teaching and reaching time is valuable, and I would much rather the reading time be spent navigating the main ideas and themes of this book instead of engaged in the intricacies of parenthetical references and other elements associated with a formal research process. For more specialized sources relative to these principles, please reference my dissertation, *Equitable Schooling for African American Students* (2018) or my book, *Equitable Schooling for African American Students* (2019), published by Lambert Academic Publishing. I will include a list of references at the end of the book, and I will be happy to delve deeper into the foundational research if your organization should see benefit in inviting me in for consulting and collaboration. Feel free to visit my website at www.infinityaspirations.com or email me at infinityaspirations@gmail.com to schedule these collaborative coaching and consulting sessions relative to building district, school, classroom culture and improving the pedagogy of stakeholder engagement.

The primary goal of this text is to provide a practical resource for identifying critical themes and issues which impact student perceptions, family participation (collaboration), and ultimately, student performance, as well as share practical and readily usable resources to address potential issues that contribute to teaching and learning challenges. The other goal is to engage educators in meaningful professional self-reflection and organizational discourse with the hope of increasing the priority for creating successful products – healthy, motivated, engaged, and well-rounded students, while at the same time reasonably balancing the priority that is currently placed on achieving a successful process – covering standards and meeting rigid bureaucratic protocols associated with the norms of high stakes testing. So, this text is intended to be as conversational as possible in hopes of increasing its practical use and application.

Choosing to place priority on identifying and effectively implementing student first strategies should help educators with establishing and maintaining effective cultures for learning that are equipped to provide a quality education and to meet students' most essential needs. Mile wide, inch deep approaches and educational gimmicks will not improve stakeholder engagement or achievement. It is a must we relentlessly put in the work to identify and utilize quality solutions. Hopefully, reading this text in a less technical format will be useful in helping educators and the educational community with achieving the intended goals. The essential remedies for improving student achievement and outcomes are simple if we place our focus and priority on the right approaches as well as use the appropriate instruments in measuring progress.

Chapter 1

Understanding and Applying the Pedagogy of Stakeholder Engagement

Prior to getting into descriptions and explanations, it is important to establish context for why this discourse matters. An organization's day-to-day governance is significantly influenced by the value and meaning it assigns its people. The value and meaning the organization gives to its people are significantly influenced by the implicit and explicit guiding principles that have been established as priority. A significant number of organizations (especially schools) allow the bureaucracy - whose protocol and expectations are shaped by the norms and influences of dominant culture – to be the compass for interacting with the diverse stakeholders in their setting. Whether these principles are right or wrong, ethical or unethical, equitable or inequitable, they will impact how people (or groups) are defined within the organization along with how protocol and policy are implemented. Subsequently, this will impact organizational equity along with stakeholder access and inclusion. Ultimately, stakeholders adopt these written or unwritten guiding principles and utilize them to unconsciously go about doing day-to-day business within their organization.

Stakeholders develop their true understanding of these guiding principles through their interaction and collaboration with leadership as well as with other members who are considered influential within the organization. Regardless of what may be written down in the organizational handbook or posted on the wall in the break room, stakeholders develop understanding of how people should be defined and the organizational guiding principles based on what they hear and what is implied by leadership and more experienced others as to how it should be. For example, while it may be written in the organization's handbook that every client, student, etc. should be treated professionally and with respect, stakeholder perceptions will be influenced more by how they see leadership and others within the organization treating certain students along with what they hear being directly and indirectly said about them. So, over time, the perceptions formulated about people and the direct and indirect values that consequently steer organizational decision-making become recognized as its standards. Essentially, it becomes commonplace for stakeholders to conduct business by defining people within the organization through a lens of those standards – which may be more favorable for some stakeholders while being less favorable for others. Relative to schooling, it is important for districts, schools, and the general educational community to be mindful of the written and unwritten principles allowed to define and guide its people because those principles shape its organizational culture.

To achieve a more fluent understanding of this book along with many of its premises, it may require some educators to reprogram or shift certain ways of thinking. It will require having a willingness to replace some things we allowed the bureaucracy to prioritize as first in our educational system with those things we allowed to slip too far down the priority list because successful achievement for all students will require changing ways of doing day-to-day business within districts and schools. For that reason, the contents of this book will not be directly focused on the methods and metrics for increasing test scores or advertising gimmicks for improving student content mastery or behavior. When you consider the principles and practices repeatedly deemed as important in our educational culture, the previous statement may seem antithetical to high student achievement. However, primarily focusing on these methods and ideologies has put the educational community in the position it is in - where many promising students with significant potential fall into an abyss of underachievement. Improving test scores, approaches to teaching the standards, student behavior, and student mastery are important components within the fabric of our educational system. Yet, these dynamics focus on improving what is measured instead of providing meaning for those who are being measured. An overabundance of pedagogical emphasis has been placed on these bureaucratic principles because we know it is professionally safe to embrace the same issues, concerns, and problems of practice that bureaucrats say are the most important things. Instead, however, we should devote our energies and efforts to the most essential component responsible for driving success - meeting the basic needs of our students. In many instances, an overzealous focus on the methods and metrics relative to testing, teaching standards, and following rigid protocol is what has contributed to the lack of engagement and support we experience with students and families today. However, using a more personable approach in connecting with students and families will improve the likelihood of creating stronger cultures. Doing this will also increase the likelihood of our achieving quality results in student achievement.

Meeting Student Needs Does Not Begin and End with Teaching Standards

Comparable to first responders, it is imperative that educators vigilantly engage with all of our students. Presumably, they are our patients, and we should provide the utmost quality care that should consist of love, understanding, nurturing, instruction, compassion, and forgiveness. Often, students will challenge our systems, authority, and even our adulthood. However, what is for certain is we cannot expect to reach "nonmainstream students" (a term discussed later in this chapter) using only at-risk student or status quo student approaches. The sooner we take ownership of that, the sooner we can effectively do something about it as an educational community because that is what will afford us the best chance of making a positive difference in the lives of ALL students we serve.

My roles in dealing with student behavior have allowed me to experience and understand the relevant needs that exist for many of our students today. The illustration on page 9 is of "Abraham Maslow's Hierarchy of Needs." If you are an educator, counselor, social worker, or are in any other human service-oriented profession, you probably recall this from psychology class. When Maslow's Hierarchy of Needs was first introduced to me in my teacher education program, I struggled to understand how to contextualize it within the premise of helping students to master standards. However, from a behavioral perspective, it is critical for us to be intentionally cognizant of Maslow's framework because a significant number of students are not getting these needs met prior to coming school. For example, many students we teach experience eviction, family displacement, and they witness influential people in their families killed, seriously injured, or incarcerated. Thus, how can we expect these students to be psychologically accountable to come to school and learn standards and achieve at their highest level if we are not first attentive and sensitive to satisfying certain deficiencies relative to their basic needs? Because of the traumas associated with many students' experiences, mastering academic standards and scoring high on tests is something they do not perceive as a critical need when compared to their other unmet needs. Realistically, we will not be able to help some students with meeting every one of their needs, but our vigilance in helping meet those we can will go a long way in building respectful and mutual relationships with them and their families.

Maslow's Hierarchy of Needs

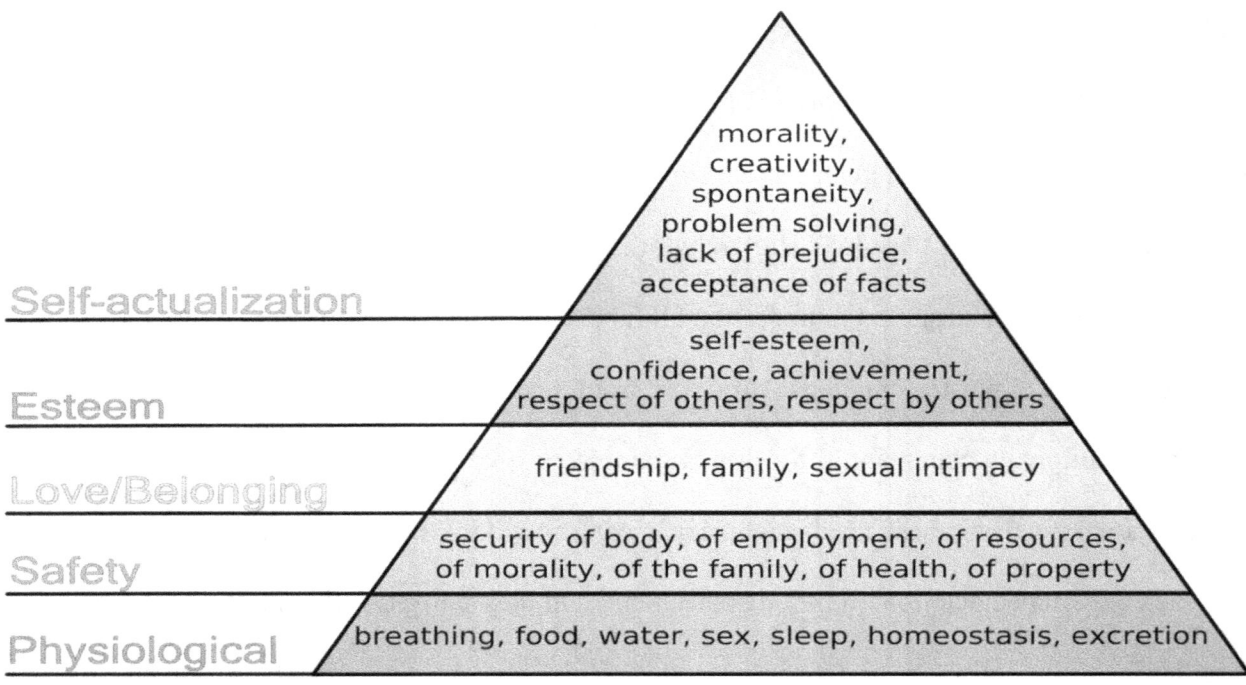

This Photo by Unknown Author is licensed under CC BY-SA

It is unfortunate that some in our profession choose to take a "not my problem" approach when it comes to meeting students' basic and personal needs in schools because they think that schools should be all about teaching academic standards and academic skills. While teaching academics is important, it is equally important that educators help students meet their basic and socioemotional needs if there is the expectation that students and families take us seriously relative to our purpose as educators. Students and parents consider educators to be disingenuous when under one breath we say we are in this profession because we love children, while under the next breath saying we are not responsible for meeting certain needs of students because we feel those needs are the responsibility of the family or home. After all, we as educators do not appreciate when it is said that teaching children to read, do math, and other tenants associated with schooling is the sole responsibility of the school because we know it is simply not an accurate statement.

While we may not be the original cause of students' problems or needs that arise, we should be willing to assume ownership in helping them to find a remedy – especially if the problem impacts the likelihood for high achievement. It should not be our place or priority to judge students, their families, circumstances, or their values. Our most essential job and focus should be to provide them with quality care in hopes of increasing their likelihood of achieving better outcomes. Thus, it is important for educators to spend quality time in defining what this role of purpose is for ourselves. If educators only see themselves as teachers of standards preparing students to pass tests, they will struggle to grow students to their maximum level of achievement. However, if educators see themselves as vessels, responsible for facilitating students' holistic learning and developmental experiences, students will have a greater chance of achieving their greatest academic and socioemotional potential. It is essential for educators to adopt this premise, but it is equally important the students and families we serve believe this to be our goal because their belief in our purpose will increase their trust in schools and open doors for building collective efficacy between homes and schools. Our intentions and purpose should be indicative in how we talk to them, how we interact with them, and especially in how we judge and evaluate them, whether in their presence or not. To be the first responders that ALL students need us to be, there is an essential step we should take to ensure the approaches and strategies existing in our toolboxes are not tainted and are targeting the needs of ALL students rather than a few.

Defining Mainstream and Nonmainstream Students

I utilize the two primary terms of "mainstream" and "nonmainstream" for distinguishing students. It is important to define and clarify these terms so they can be referenced and applied with the highest degree of utility possible. In special education, the term "mainstream" generally refers to ensuring students with Individualized Education Programs (IEPs) are placed in their least restrictive environments (LREs). In the special education arena, mainstreaming students is essential for building their efficacy and contributing to their academic growth. Obviously, all students in schools are not in special education, but I believe it is important to correlate this ideology when considering the diverse population of students in school communities.

There are a significant number of students who come from married two parent homes. Divorce rates and the overall increase in single parent households have decreased the percentage of students living in married two parent households, but dominant culture has programmed society into believing this traditional family structure is most appropriate and, and therefore is mainstream. So, students who come from this family structure usually have unwritten perceptual advantages over those who do not because the two-parent family structure is viewed more favorably according to the norms and standards of mainstream dominant culture. In certain districts and schools, students who come from married two parent homes are unconsciously perceived as the likely higher performing, more obedient students because in many instances the implicit guiding assertion is that these students' home structures most closely resemble and align with the structures and expectations of the educational setting. In other words, many students coming from this type of household structure or norms are often given an unwritten benefit of the doubt because of the subliminal perception about kids who come from married two parent home structures. Additionally, because there are two parents in the home, these families often have a capacity to be more visible and engaged in the school – which subsequently benefits their kids in having better learning and social experiences in the school system. Therefore, I define these students as mainstream students because the dynamics of their home lives better equip them for success in the typical school setting.

It is not to suggest that these students are better or smarter than students who come from a different type of setting. Additionally, it is not to suggest that ALL the students who identify with the above descriptions will be successful in school. However, because of who and what influences today's mainstream schools, the embedded perception is that mainstream students come to school equipped with more of the precursors needed for survival and success in the mainstream school settings, settings that are most often grounded and influenced by the norms of White privilege and dominant culture. Because they come from households with structures and systems resembling these school settings, many of these students are more likely to be compatible with teachers and staff as well as knowledgeable of the unwritten norms of expectation and consequence relative to the school setting.

On the other hand, our communities also consist of students who come from homes where there is one parent who is the sole breadwinner or where there is someone other than their biological mother or father as their guardian. Because of being the only breadwinner or having the unexpected task of parenting placed on them, these parents or guardians may work a lot as well as have more individual responsibilities to ensure household obligations are met. Consequently, some systems existing in this type of home structure may not resemble that of a home where there are two biological parents. Additionally, there are students who come from homes where their parents or guardians have had negative or unproductive experiences in their dealings with the educational, financial, legal, or healthcare systems. Some students falling into this category also may come from homes involving contentious divorce, and consequently, they experienced unexpected lifestyle changes in addition to other associated experiential traumas. In other words, there are students who come from untraditional and nonmainstream homes where these along with other life altering experiences consistently impact their daily lives. I define these students as nonmainstream students because a high percentage of their lifestyles are not compatible with the structures, systems, and expectations associated with the mainstream school setting. Because of the differences between these students and the mainstream students, who come from homes fitting the acceptable dominant culture power and influence structure, their habits, mannerisms, and lifestyles are often questioned and scrutinized more frequently within many school settings. It is not to suggest that just because nonmainstream students come from a different type of home setting than mainstream students they are not smart or capable of being cooperative within the context of learning. However, because their household settings function differently from the systems and structures within many schools, it increases their likelihood of being involved in teacher or staff conflicts or cultural disconnect because their habits, mannerisms, and everyday experiences naturally contrast that of the school environment.

It is easy for the education community to say the politically correct thing. A statement which says, "We view all students through the same lens regardless of their race or home status." However, years of data show that in numerous school settings, many students and families are stigmatized as uncaring because they fall outside of the norms of what the school perceives to be appropriate. For example, if there is difficulty in getting in touch with a single parent or families with an untraditional household structure, they are often labeled as uncaring or apathetic. A similar reaction occurs when these families lack involvement in school activities such as teacher meetings, PTA meetings, etc. While there are irresponsible parents and caregivers within our schools, it is also probable that obstacles such as these exist because of the differences in structure and responsibility in a one-parent untraditional (nonmainstream) home versus a two-parent traditional (mainstream) home. The unfortunate consequence is some students and families are misperceived, adversely labeled, and frowned upon in educational settings because of the differences in their lifestyles. Often, the mainstream school's perspective asserts that if we cannot get in touch with the family or parents when we need them, it is obvious the parents or family do not care about the child or his success in school. Further, a school may conclude that if these parents hardly ever attend school events or meetings, the child has minimal support, and the family is unconcerned. Consequently, students who come from these types of family dynamics are often the unfortunate beneficiaries of the same types of label and consequent misperceptions by multiple staff members within schools.

Now that these terms have been defined, please remember these important points. First, just because students come from a certain type of background does not guarantee they will be successful relative to their performance and achievement in school. Nonmainstream students have just as much potential to perform and be successful in school as mainstream students because a high amount of student success is determined by their motivation. Student motivation will impact how much value is placed on academic success as well as the amount of effort put towards accomplishing tasks. However, it is important to realize that the culture and climate significantly contribute to shaping student motivation in addition to perceptions. So, students' perceptions subsequently influence their motivation and desire to be successful. Second, while I am not suggesting that student backgrounds should be used to label students' abilities to be successful or unsuccessful, I am saying that it is important to understand the hidden and unhidden influences organizational norms have on students' abilities to learn. Thus, if districts and schools consciously or unconsciously devalue or ignore students' experiences and norms, we run the risk of using irrelevant data and ineffective approaches in determining how to improve their achievement.

The 'At-Risk' vs. 'NonMainstream' Terminology

Part of the way we as educators begin to take ownership is to take responsibility for any unclear messaging, a point that will be addressed more in a later chapter. However, if we, as educators, expect others to take what we do more seriously, our messaging needs to be more consistent with the overall goal of student achievement. The purpose of this section is to investigate and reflect upon the term "at risk" in hopes of creating greater messaging clarity in our purpose.

As previously referenced, many of today's students do not come to school saying, "Yes Ma'am" and "No Sir," wearing their hair in traditionally conservative styles, or having gotten the standard 8 to 10 hours sleep the night before. Further, many students today come to school without having sat at a table with their two-parent family, siblings, and a pet to fellowship for dinner. Also, a significant number of students come to school without having read a book the night before, or without having had time to themselves because of having to babysit younger siblings. Many students we serve today have relatives who are incarcerated or have had bad experiences with institutions (education, marriage, divorce, family court, criminal justice, etc.). The point is a significant number of our students fit into one or more of these categories. As educators, it is important we take ownership and responsibility of the premise that ALL students have the capacity to be brilliant regardless of what category they may fall into. We also should be realistic in understanding that there are fewer model high achieving students (mainstream students) today - students coming from the two parent homes with traditional hairstyles, conservative fitted clothing, and anticipated to comply with all rules and expectations the first time they are given. Essentially, many students today are the exact opposite of the previously mentioned qualities and at first glance would not be perceived as having the capacity to be exemplary or high achieving. However, it is important to realize that these students are just as brilliant as the model of the "high achieving" student many educators envision in their heads. However, these students will only realize and display their ability if we tap into their brilliance in uniquely effective ways.

It is unfortunate that the bureaucracy even uses the term "at risk" for students who fall into these categories. As an educator, I respectfully have a problem with this terminology because I personally think it implies and sends the wrong message to stakeholders. First, think about the connotation associated with the term "at risk." Does the term make you think or perceive in a positive context? Second, if schools are sanctuaries for empowerment, enrichment, and achievement, how does using a term such as at risk suggest we are empowering and enriching students towards achievement as it relates to learning and development? What does the term imply about who we teach and how we are teaching? The fact that students are at school should make them the exact opposite of at-risk. So, why would we reference students who are a part of our learning cultures in this way? Personally, I prefer to reference the students who fall into any of the previously mentioned categories (or any categories implying dysfunction) as nonmainstream students instead of at-risk students. Therefore, many students we serve and educate today are nonmainstream students instead of at-risk students. Now, some may read this section and believe many of the things mentioned is what is wrong with our students as well as education today. Some may feel we are allowing society to manipulate and ultimately dictate the changes to our educational system. If someone is drawing that conclusion, it would be accurate because it is necessary to adapt and adjust so we can accommodate and meet the needs of the student populations we serve. If our students are a part of a society that consists of an ever-changing diversity of cultures and perspectives, what benefit would it be to provide a rigid educational system that shows little or no indication of trying to adjust in meeting students where they are? So, to look at this from a context of adjusting and accommodating our system (relative to terminology, programs, and services) is accurate, but to perceive it as a negative thing is counterproductive.

It is important we realize that there are some of the traditional model rigidities within our education system that create inequitable circumstances for many students today. The refusal to modify and adjust certain institutions and systems within our society continues to perpetuate cyclical disadvantages among certain groups and classes of people – which significantly influences why certain things remain the way they are relative to achievement. So, for us to place blame or have a pity party about why so few students are in the high achievement category or for us to challenge why it is necessary to modify "status quo" systems which have been in place for too long decreases the likelihood of engaging in constructive discourse that can potentially move us closer to meeting the needs of ALL students. Further, engaging in pity party or blame game discourse relinquishes educators from their responsibility of effectively using creative autonomy in finding constructive strategies and solutions to grow these students. In sum, words plant the seeds, and it is important our terms and vernacular send a clear message of high expectation and achievement. Doing so will naturally activate our creativity as well as our instructional strategies in doing the same.

Cultures That Influence Achievement

I use two diagrams to illustrate the difference between creating impersonable metrics-standards driven cultures and more personable student and stakeholder driven cultures in districts and schools. The major difference to pay attention to is what or who is in the center of each diagram. The first diagram on page 20 shows a framework of a standards-metrics driven culture. In many districts and schools, curriculum standards, their associated metrics (testing, diagnostic testing, etc.), and dominant culture behavior policy influenced by White privilege are the standards which most substantially influence the educational culture. This represents a standards-metrics driven culture because these principles are the major priorities, and they govern the culture as well as the direct and indirect policies associated with schooling. In this type of setting, schools and districts spend the largest chunk of time attempting to figure out how to improve students through mastering standards and enforcing the metrics. Because so much time is spent on the formalities of standards, protocol, and associated metrics, the human elements (students, parents, teachers, staff, and social capital (people of a student's community who have positive influence over them)) are on the outskirts of the triangle. This creates an engagement disconnect between stakeholders because a high amount of focus is placed on standards, protocol, and metrics associated with bureaucratic expectations. Because mainstream students have more familiarity with these types of systems and structures, they are more likely to be the students who make good grades, score high on tests, and behave appropriately in a standards and metrics engagement model. Also, one of the parents of mainstream students is probably more likely to have experienced some degree of success in this type of setting. Because these parents and their children experience success in this type of setting, the parents as well as the social capital of these students usually are more likely to buy into the culture. Therefore, the parents and social capital for these students will likely be more engaged and supportive in this type of setting in comparison to students and families who have less familiarity or success with this type of setting. It is important to reiterate and clarify that the reference to standards (in this model) is more than academic curriculum. It also includes the associated policy and protocol associated with behavior.

The term "standards-driven" is also applicable when considering behavioral policies and other protocol that represent influential staples within an educational culture. It is important to note a considerable amount of "standards-driven" protocol, whether academic or behavioral, are a byproduct of the White privilege perspective of "good" rule or "good" order – which correlates with having authority and power. For example, in many elementary school settings, the standard expectation for students walking in the hallway is to walk in a line and to not talk. I have experienced instances where students caught talking (even whispering), receive negative reprimands and harsh consequences for doing so. Additionally, the teacher whose class is permitted to talk in the hallway is perceived as a subpar classroom manager or has an inability to follow school protocol. Understandably, the concepts of rules and order are essential to teach students, and there are definite instances where rules and expectations may need to be non-negotiable (e.g. safety issues). However, an environment which places rigid emphasis on reprimanding students for whispering or talking softly in a hallway line while transitioning to lunch, recess, or other routine activities would be an example of a standards and metrics focused culture because adherence to the standard takes noticeable precedence over the needs or interests of students. Similarly, from an academic context, the school or classroom environment that gives considerably more recognition to honor roll students or students who have the highest test scores (which quite often are the same students) than students who simply brought up grades and made improvements would also be an example of a standards and metrics focused culture.

Standards & Metrics Focused Engagement Approach

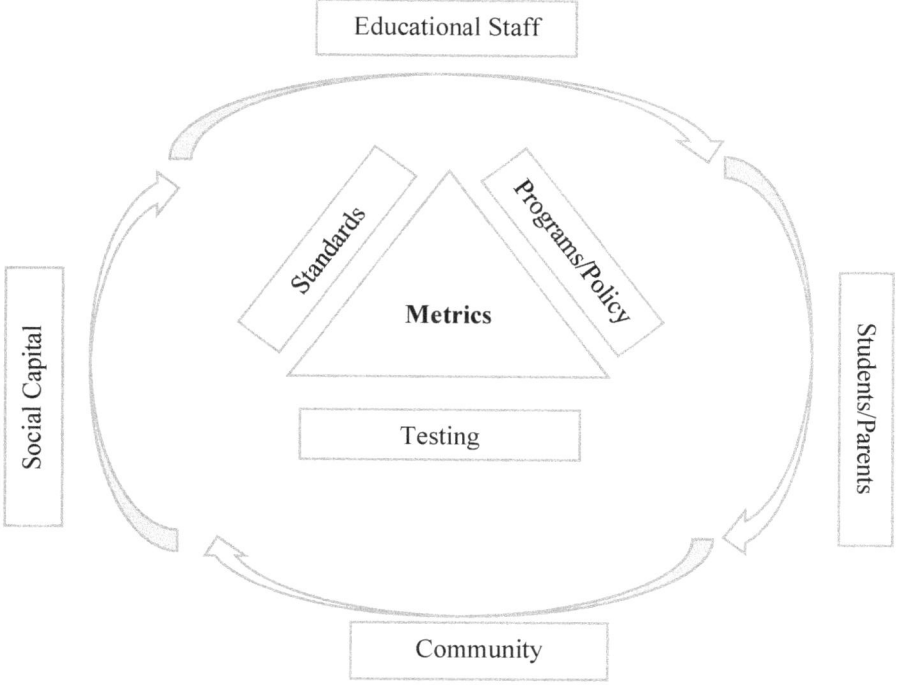

In a perfect world, all home and community support would resemble mainstream students who are accustomed to school norms, but the reality is this group often represents a smaller constituency of stakeholders in many districts and schools. In many instances, nonmainstream students, their parents, and community supporters have not experienced the same level of consistent success in schooling. So, a standards and metrics focused culture will be more of a challenge for them to embrace and excel in. While parents and social capital for these students want to see them do well, their lack of familiarity and lack of interest in the standards and metrics used to govern these environments deter their motivation to be supportive or involved. The fact is if they nor their children have been successful in this type of environment, it is less likely they will buy into engaging with their full support because standards, protocol, and metrics will never be more important to them than the overall well-being of their children. Thus, as long as these stakeholders feel that standards, curriculum, testing, and policy are the focus of the culture within the educational community, a culture which has already not produced a high level of success for many of them as well as their child, it is highly unlikely they will fully buy into it with active engagement or support. If this is true, it also increases the likelihood that the children these parents have influence over will also not be fully engaged in this type of setting.

Consequently, maintaining a standards and metrics focused culture will perpetuate the cycle of the same high achieving students while doing little to improve achievement for many other students. Further, this type of culture frames things from more of a context of "us against them" instead of a context of partnership. It always seems to generate a narrative that pits districts and schools versus parents, homes, and communities – which produces numerous complaints, counter complaints, and empty promises. For example, districts and schools assert that many parents are not involved the way they should be, and arbitrarily conclude that they (the parents) do not care. Conversely, many parents and the communities claim the only time they hear from districts and schools is when they have an agenda, it is time for a conference, or if their child is in trouble. To these stakeholders, it appears as though districts and schools do not care. The outcome is that both sides only deal with each other at surface level or in abrasive ways such as artificial smiles and salutations during encounters while making derogatory comments in private or parents coming to school to curse out staff members. So, while the standards and metrics driven culture may be deemed as important in some arenas within the educational community, it is less important to nonmainstream students, their parents, social capital, and communities.

Stakeholder Engagement Approach

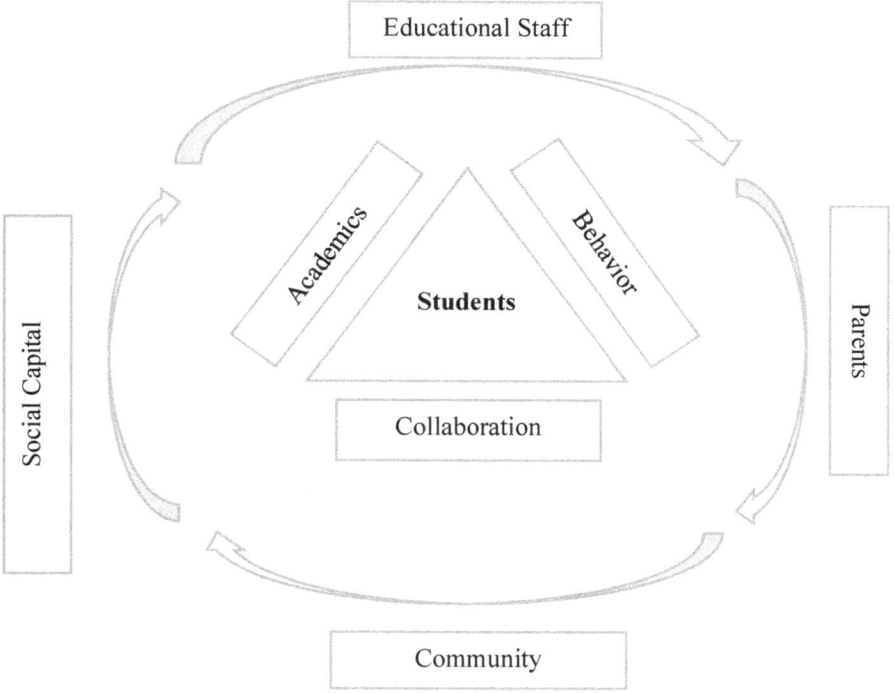

The above diagram illustrates the framework for the "The Stakeholder Engagement Approach," also referenced as the "pedagogy of stakeholder engagement." In this diagram, the most essential stakeholder, the student, is in the center, and all other components revolve around the student. Advocating this type of culture means everything (standards, behavior protocol, data, collaboration, etc.) should be geared toward the needs of the student. Additionally, you will notice that metrics are not present in this framework. The thought behind this model is when the students are placed at the center with everything and everyone else revolving around them to meet their needs, the metrics, test scores, and other associated bureaucratic expectations are more likely to take care of themselves. Essentially, the Stakeholder Engagement Approach emphasizes the idea that the more student needs are met through a collaborative effort of human resources, the better they will perform and the more cohesive the overall environment will be in accomplishing this task. For example, instead of immediate disciplinary actions – which quite often seek to remove the student from the classroom setting - the student needing behavior intervention due to behavior challenges would begin immediate positive collaboration with human resources (staff, parents, community, and social capital) at school and home. Ultimately, the goal of this type of model is to build efficacy and agency in the student through student reflection, progress monitoring, and collaboration with more experienced others. Further, this approach builds a team of support around the student and equips him with the tools to become more self-sufficient in taking an ownership role in his growth and development. This type of culture requires an all-inclusive and bias-free accountability system for ensuring that students' needs are met. Whether behavioral or academic, students' needs drive the collaboration, the data, as well as the plans of action in this framework rather than the needs for fulfilling the standards, metrics, and protocol.

Some may declare their educational setting already has a student-centered focus. However, one of the intended purposes of this chapter is to urge districts and schools to be careful not to base their success relative to stakeholder engagement or student success on test results or other bureaucratic accolades they may have achieved. Doing so actually perpetuates the standards and metrics engagement approach and embraces the mile wide and inch deep approaches which lessen the likelihood of longer-term success and achievement for certain students or groups of students who, in most cases, are already marginalized. So, it is essential for educational communities to thoroughly investigate their cultures below the surface because that is where the standards, protocols, and policies stifling achievement for many students can reside if there is an absence of deep organizational reflection, evaluation, or assessment.

It goes without saying there are an abundance of curriculum materials, behavior programs, computer applications, etc. adopted by districts or schools under the pretense of being student–centered. I am not saying these programs do not have the potential or capacity to meet the needs of your students. However, implementing programs and resources into an educational community is not what makes them student-centered, create a student-centered culture, or create a culture rich with stakeholder engagement. If there is no local process in place to evaluate the effectiveness of programs, protocol, and resources, it is possible for these resources to do more harm than good relative to meeting students' needs. Therefore, it is essential for districts, schools, and the education community to frequently evaluate and assess resources and practices to ensure their effectiveness for meeting the needs of ALL students within their educational setting. It is suggested to utilize the themes identified in the next several chapters to assist with this process.

Points of Reflection

Brilliance in students is not determined by who says, "Yes Sir" or "No Ma'am." Many brilliant students come to school with their pants worn below their waists and have untraditional hairstyles. Further, there are a lot of brilliant students who come to school and do not have opportunities to read to one of their parents or for one of their parents to read to them. A significant number of brilliant students come to school and are responsible for caring for younger siblings just as much as they care for themselves. Today's societal implications mean that many students do not come from the traditional home settings often revered by the dominant culture influenced settings of schools. It is important the hidden and unhidden norms and expectations of districts and schools create a welcoming culture for ALL students. This is the only way to shift the achievement paradigm so ALL students and families feel supported, motivated, and engaged in maximizing their achievement.

Our pedagogy relative to districts, schools, and classrooms should be less focused on improving things and more focused on improving people. Standards, metrics, and everything that comes along with them are the things. Students, their families, teachers, and staff are living, breathing stakeholders – the human resources. If we spend more time trying to improve our pedagogy to better the engagement of the things while spending minimal time bettering our engagement of the people, we will continue reaping similar results. If our approaches give focus to the things instead of the people, our approaches will objectify the human elements and subsequently alienate stakeholders as well as their willingness to be genuinely and meaningfully engaged. It is how we engage and improve our relationships with stakeholders that will change things for the better.

There are numerous standards, curriculum, programs, and their associated metrics that have the potential to add value to educational communities. However, just because they are championed as research-based, tested, or proven does not guarantee they will reach all students and achieve effective results in unique, educational settings. Simply putting resources into place without having an evaluation or assessment system will perpetuate mile wide and inch deep approaches. To determine whether standards, protocol, programs, policies, and their associated metrics are effective in meeting the needs for diverse groups of learners, schools and districts need to put meaningful effort into evaluating how well these resources are working to meet student needs in their unique settings. What works successfully in one setting is not guaranteed to work as successfully for ALL students in another setting. If educational communities do not have a plan for evaluating and assessing the effectiveness of curriculum, programs, or policies, they have no means of certifying whether these resources are meeting the needs of ALL students and improving stakeholder engagement. Continuing to utilize resources and approaches without evaluating or assessing their level of effectiveness for students is like throwing a dart at a dart board while blind folded. If meeting the needs of ALL students is the goal, it is necessary to evaluate and assess each tool, resource, and approach being utilized to ensure the desired goal is being achieved.

Chapter 1 Reflection Questions

What percentage of the school day is driven by academic content and standards?

What percentage of the school day is driven by meeting the socioemotional and nonacademic developmental needs of students?

What percentage of staff serves as coaches or mentors for at least five students and their families?

Is the class/school/district culture more stakeholder engagement-focused or standards and metrics focused? What evidence supports your conclusion?

Setting	**Stakeholder or Standards/Metrics**	**Evidence**
Class		
School		
District		

Chapter 2

Messages Matters

Having been a part of the educational system for over 20 years, I have witnessed many local, state, and federal changes. I have often found myself wondering whether changes in curriculum, protocol, policies, and the associated metrics are implemented for the purpose of better equipping students to become self-sufficient contributors in creating better lives for themselves, or more about making things easier for bureaucracy. While changes in education, both large and small, have been frequent, there is always the resonating theme of, "It's not enough." Since higher test scores always seem to dominate the forefront, the typical answer for addressing issues in education mostly has been the same – add more metrics of accountability to education and educators.

Regardless of how many times the curriculum, standardized tests, diagnostic tests, or academic programs change, the claim still exists that many students are being left behind, or they are not experiencing the level of success in relation to their higher performing counterparts. Moreover, the claim for those students who 'meet' the standards of the state or district tests is that many of them are still not learning at the potential for which they are capable. Complaints about student progress are ongoing in education, yet much of the bureaucratic emphasis relative to changes in schooling has focused on standards, testing, and metrics. However, more efforts, funding, and energy need to be put towards non-academic programs and services that contribute to meeting the socioemotional and other developmental needs of students. When we as an educational community continue with business as usual, focusing more heavily on standards, protocol, testing, and metrics and less on other essential needs of students, we send a clear message to students as well as all other pertinent stakeholders with respect to where priorities lie. Because of factors such as these, less time and emphasis are placed on changing school climate and culture.

Classroom and School Culture

Historically, the bureaucracy has attempted to hold districts and schools accountable for underperformance through ultimatums, threats, and ridicule (e.g. rating schools with letter grades, etc.). Seemingly, these types of tactics give explanation to why most of the notable changes within education frequently occur in standards and testing. Since testing and standards are the notable metrics used by the bureaucracy, many districts and schools place greater emphasis on these components because some believe meeting adequate achievement on high stakes accountability testing will improve the narrative and eliminate the underachievement conversation. This approach is so engrained in our educational system that districts and schools implement classroom, curriculum, and behavior policy using the same tactics as the bureaucracy - threats, ultimatums, and ridicule. From the beginning of our country, these techniques have been utilized as weapons to perpetuate authority, power, and privilege.

However, these methods should provoke several questions. First, if the claim is students are still not achieving to their potential, why is the emphasis continuously placed on the same things - changing standards, testing metrics, and maintaining rigid policies that often marginalize the same groups of students? Second, why does the educational community choose to buy into the same tactics (threats, pressure, and ridicule) in pursuit of achieving a different result, especially when evidence suggests these approaches are counterproductive? In the many interactions I have had with educators, it seems a significant number of us are critical of the bureaucratic approaches for evaluating teachers and schools, but many districts, schools, and educators utilize similar approaches to evaluate students as well as families within their educational settings. Third, has changing the standards or testing improved student engagement, student depth of learning, or increased home-school interaction? Fourth, have the blanket zero tolerance behavior policies utilized in many schools created the positive change in students – especially the ones they were intended to impact? Fifth, if intimidation tactics have worked and there is evidence of such a drastic change for the better, why do we continuously hear the same direct or indirect complaint – "It is not enough?" The most important question is this: "What message do our approaches send to the students and families we serve in these schools?"

Regardless of our opinions about certain families and their values, they show a degree of trust in us simply by sending their best and most prized product to our districts and schools daily–their children. Their children are the stakeholders who should be the most actively engaged in our districts and schools, and they are the reason our profession exists. However, do our programs, policies, and protocols send the message that they are first, or do they show that achieving standards, higher test scores, and all other associated metrics are first? Meeting students' holistic developmental needs will make them more effective and engaged learners, and it will send the message that students are the priority. Seemingly, placing emphasis on the same thing we have done for years does not appear to be the way forward for meeting student needs and elevating achievement. One of the most important things we can do as educators in promoting student achievement is provide academic and behavioral learning experiences that increase students' engagement in their personal reflection because experiences such as these are beneficial for them in assessing their personal growth. Arguably, creating equitable academic and discipline systems is essential for building these meaningful school and class cultures that set the tone relative to messaging and create smoother transitions into their ability to master curriculum. For this to occur, it is necessary for our messaging to be consistent, using clear words, programs, plans, and overall actions.

School Discipline Culture – Messages of Confinement or Empowerment?

School discipline is a major area where disconnect, disruption, and unclear messaging occur in schools because discipline protocol heavily influences climate and culture messaging. Additionally, it is the area where many districts, schools, and educators assert their personal biases and subjective perceptions when it comes to determining the magnitude and subsequent consequences of student behavior. For example, one educator may interpret verbal rebuttal as disrespectful whereas another educator may not. Moreover, school discipline is also the area where messaging can be the most unclear and significantly damage attempts to build stronger cultures. This is where all stakeholders within an educational community need to take a self-inventory relative to their role and influence in setting the tone regarding the culture within their educational settings. It is essential for educators to take ownership of initiating this process and accept the responsibility for doing much of the heavy lifting in creating equitable cultures.

Everyone in the educational community probably agrees about the influences that behavior and discipline have on school culture, climate, and effectiveness. However, some also do not assume that as being their responsibility. The educators who feel their only roles in schools are to teach standards and do morning, lunch, and afternoon duties have a smaller likelihood of affecting change in student discipline - especially if they take that perspective when interacting with nonmainstream students. Relative to school culture and discipline, mentoring students and teaching character is more important in building an effective educational setting than standards, procedures, and protocol. However, it is also important that our mentorship and teaching of character promote reasonable tolerance as well as messages that build a nurturing, constructive culture instead of a condescending, abusive, and destructive one. As it relates to school discipline culture messaging, the intention is not to jump on the "Kids are acting up and nothing is being done about it" or "We can't do our jobs effectively because of student behavior" bandwagons. Therefore, it is important to clarify and provide further context for what is meant by climate and culture messaging in the areas of behavior and discipline.

It is important we understand that engaging in meaningful discourse relative to behavior and discipline should not consist of complaining about outcomes. For example, a teacher who sends a student to the office should not complain because the student did not receive the outcome the teacher expected. First, that approach seeks to point the finger outward before looking inward. Further, this approach contradicts the message of promoting self-reflection, which is what we expect our students to be able to do. Secondly, however, once a student is sent to the office, it is out of the hands of the classroom. So, once a referral is written and a student is sent to the office, the primary control of assigning the consequence defaults to administration. A teacher sending a student to an administrator and then complaining about the subsequent consequence is futile, and it also signals a message of starved collaboration between classrooms and administrators. Third, placing emphasis on severity sends the message to many students that teachers and staff member's primary concern is to inflict punishment, pain, or seek vengeance, which often does not contribute to improving behavior or building positive messaging. We should consider equitable approaches that give more priority to reinforcing responsible behavior while also showing tolerance for considering students' individual needs.

Because so many of our students come from home structures and environments different from that of school, their experiences will shape their perception to view certain actions differently. For example, students who come from home settings or communities where they witnessed family members arrested or mistreated by American systems (legal, financial, healthcare, or educational) will view certain consequences from different lenses than other students. So, it is probable that engaging in power struggles with them, being overzealous with zero-tolerance policy or assigning them to traditional in-school suspension (ISS), out-of-school suspension (OSS), or detention structures are less likely to have a positive impact or outcome on their willingness to reflect or change their behavior.

While zero-tolerance may be necessary for certain behavioral infractions, the "My way or the highway" approach does not represent an adequate approach for behavior planning in the same way it is not considered adequate for academic planning. Certain situations will call for zero-tolerance policy as well as the implementation of those types of associated consequences. It is common sense that major discipline infractions that require more assertive measures will occur within educational settings. However, the suggestion here is zero-tolerance-like approaches are often overused when dealing with many students either out of convenience, apathy, or because there is a lack of tolerance and concern for the welfare of students who are assigned those consequences (hopefully not the latter).

Students mature and progress at different rates behaviorally in the same way they progress at different rates academically. How can we expect all students to be successful when valuable time is spent planning for academics and standards-based components while minimal time is spent planning for behavioral and socioemotional development? We know the whole student will be a participant in our educational settings, and we know that those same students will have needs for improving behavior in the same way they will have needs for improving their academics. Thus, it is not sensible to give the impression of being well-planned for teaching students if adequate planning, preparation, and subsequent assessments have not been considered for both areas (behavior and academics). It is imperative we send the message that we care about meeting all of students' needs instead of only caring about the needs causing us the least inconvenience or the needs we feel are most crucial for passing the test. This is where many districts and schools should be mindful not to gravitate towards the standards and metrics focused approach because both dimensions (academics and behavior) should be considered with the same degree of seriousness and consideration.

Year after year the same programs, protocol, and policies are implemented relative to addressing behavior and discipline while all types of new assessments, strategies, and modifications are implemented to ensure academic standards are covered. The unfortunate result is the same students continue underperforming and failing because we as an educational community devote a considerable amount of our time changing curriculum standards and associated metrics while devoting lesser time to socioemotional and character development. If we care about students, we will be reflective about the message we send when ISS, OSS, detention, and overzealous zero-tolerance policies are consistently overused as remedies for disciplining the same groups of students.

The National Center for Educational Statistics (2015) shows that minority students (specifically, Hispanic and African American) are most frequently suspended in schools. The same research indicates that Hispanic and African American students have the lowest graduation rates in comparison to their counterparts. A significant number of minority students are also in the nonmainstream student category. So, if ISS, OSS, and detention platforms most significantly impact these students, what message are they receiving from consistent interaction with these platforms, and how is it improving their ability to develop and achieve? Further, what message are these families receiving from us relative to our purpose when they have frequent encounters with detentions or suspensions that do not produce any evidence of improving their child's behavior? Some will contend they are learning that inappropriate behavior has consequences and that issuing these discipline alternatives show students their behavior needs to change. However, I challenge that notion from two perspectives. First, in many instances, rules, procedures, and protocol are hyper-interpreted for nonmainstream and marginalized students. In other words, a mainstream student who never gets in trouble and talks out of turn is more likely to get a less harsh disciplinary consequence than a nonmainstream student who has had previous disciplinary infractions. Scenarios such as the one above is directly impacted by bias, and bias should not be a center of influence when considering how to equitably interact with students (more about this in Chapter 3). Second, if the same students frequent ISS, OSS, detention, or any other program without showing improvement and our approaches within our educational settings do not change, how can it be said there is an expectation for their behavior to change when our strategies and approaches never do? As an educational community, we should care enough to look at the right data, ask the right questions, and take an honest inventory about the answers. Failure to do so perpetuates a cycle of inequitable educational cultures that reinforce an ongoing agenda of contention and confinement instead of liberation and empowerment.

Meaningful Engagement Fosters Equity and Empowerment

Whether learning experiences are for refinement, reinforcement, remediation, or reprimand, they should promote student efficacy and self-regulation through allowing students to engage in a reflective process. These types of experiences cultivate mindsets and promote self-empowerment because students will be better equipped to measure and connect the expectations of the learning experience to how they should adjust their output so they can achieve greater success. In simpler terms, a classroom or disciplinary learning experience should be focused on meaningfully engaging students in reflecting on what they can or have learned from the experience so they might grow. This should also consist of the student interacting with social capital and mentors as a way of providing constructive support and guidance during the reflective process. It is easy to see this process unfold in many schools when it comes to academic learning experiences, but it is much more convoluted when it comes to disciplinary learning experiences. The topic of evaluating disciplinary practices and procedures becomes contentious at times because some think worrying about discipline should not be educators' tasks. This attitude reinforces the standards first approach to schooling and is why many students fall through the cracks. However, school programs and procedures should be inclusive for the constructive and holistic development of ALL students. If the academic and disciplinary programs as well as procedures at schools exist to target meeting the needs of only mainstream students, performance and achievement disparities will continue to be most prevalent with the students who need help the most.

Programs, protocols, and policies in districts, schools, and classrooms should exist to constructively develop students. Specifically, establishing academic and discipline programs and procedures is essential for encouraging progress, maintaining accountability, and order. However, it is equally important to ensure these programs and procedures align with a productive intended purpose and send the right message to students and families. On the discipline side of things, detention, ISS, and OSS are frequently used platforms in a lot of schools, but they are also the source of conflict and disconnect between many students, homes, and schools, often due to misperceived or unclear messaging. When discipline conflicts occur, the easy and convenient narrative is to write students or parents off as not wanting to take responsibility for the identified behavior. However, clinging to such a narrative also sends the message that neither the student or their family has a concern about growth or being more successful. It may be true the student is receiving detention, ISS, or OSS because he violated a rule, procedure, or policy, but that does not necessarily mean he did so because of a lack of concern for following protocol. This might be the first thought for some educators, especially if the student is a repeat offender to any disciplinary procedures. However, if educators draw this conclusion without the benefit of using professional discretion or reflection, their behavior would be just as irresponsible as what they are accusing these students and their parents of doing. As was previously discussed, many students we serve come from homes of different structures than school. So, it may take additional time for them to accept, develop, and model certain behaviors and habits. However, their inability to do so based on a given timeline does not mean they (or their families) do not care about improving. Especially in disciplinary circumstances, it is extremely important for educational communities to send the message to students and their families that the common goal is for student growth and development, despite how long it may take for the growth and development to take place. However, this message often gets lost in the emotions, indifference, and biases involved in disciplinary situations.

The educational community should assume the leadership role in making sure the appropriate message is relayed to students and families when discipline situations arise. If we are quick to apply a deficit way of thinking relative to certain students and hastily draw the conclusion of "That child just doesn't care," or "That parent just doesn't care about her child," without taking the time to seek further knowledge about the student, their family, their circumstances, and how our pedagogy and protocol influences student behavior, we are sending a clear message that following standards of behavior protocol is more important than discovering how to make each child more successful. It is time for us as an educational community to abandon this way of thinking because it places a barrier between many of our students, parents, and schools.

The obvious preference is for students to be actively involved and engaged in the regular school and classroom setting. However, the educational community should not view ISS, OSS, detention, and other disciplinary procedures as dumping grounds for students who have discipline problems because it is not beneficial for their growth. Ultimately, we should take a responsible inventory in considering whether these discipline approaches are doing more to contribute to the school-to-prison pipeline or the refine-and-empower pipeline – the pathway where ALL educational programs provide constructive student feedback which gives them accountable ownership in reforming and shaping their own behaviors. Assigning a student to ISS, giving them work to complete while there, and chastising them when they are off task will do little to provide constructive feedback essential for changing the student's behavior. Programs such as ISS should go further by providing constructive, individualized student support and feedback through establishing a collaborative system of student accountability where students are engaged in assuming a role of responsibility for changing their behavior. A student may not be ready to assume full responsibility for changing her behavior. However, similar to how educators are expected to scaffold learning experiences academically, we should also practice the same standard when it comes to student behavior and socioemotional development because many students will need repeated practice with mastering certain skills and habits.

Educators must be willing to reflect and consider whether our programs lend themselves to improving or diminishing student motivation relative to succeeding in school. It is no coincidence the same constituency of students who are most frequently suspended also represent the same demographic of students who consistently underperform academically and behaviorally in schools. It is also not coincidence that the same contingency of students who are most frequently suspended in schools represent the same contingency of the country's most incarcerated demographic.

Correlations in findings such as these represent a systemic problem of practice and messaging we cannot ignore or attempt to explain away. If we do not take diligent accountability in finding solutions to these challenges, we send the message that we do not care about the welfare or success of these groups of students. If we send or suggest the message we do not care, how can we expect them to be motivated to care and work hard for us? Regardless of how some may try to spin it, much of this failure resides within the educational community's way of doing things, and blame should not be conveniently assigned to students and their families. If detention, ISS, OSS, and other such alternatives are to be incorporated in schools, they need to be utilized for serving a specific purpose relative to improving and growing the students who must interact with these platforms. If discipline platforms such as these remain in existence within schools without improving the students who are most involved in them, continuing their use in the same way sends the wrong message. Consequently, relaying a message of apathy or unconcern will create more cultural challenges instead of cultural improvements. Further, if district and school data indicate that ISS, OSS, and detention are proving ineffective in growing and refining the students being served, yet these platforms are continuously utilized in the same way, these alternatives cannot be interpreted or represented any differently from the solitary confinement or general population like settings resembling the prison system.

Misbehavior Is Not a Scapegoat

It is inaccurate and the wrong message for any educators to say we cannot do our jobs because of student behavior. The capacity to educate is broad in scope, and students of today need to be educated on many things – academics, rules, technology, conduct, as well as character development. So, for anyone to say they cannot do their job because of student misbehavior is also saying the task of educating children is limited in scope. This goes back to the suggestion that educators' only roles are to teach standards and perform their assigned duties. If educators send this message, it will create more of a challenge to get student and family buy-in (especially for non-mainstream students) because it gives the impression that educators are only interested in meeting needs they think are important rather than the specific and unique needs that exist for each student. What you teach or educate a student on at any given moment may not correspond with your agenda, preference, lesson plan, etc., but there is always a teachable moment, especially since many students come to our districts, schools, and classrooms lacking academically as well as socioemotionally. If the dialogue of blaming students and their families drives classroom and school discipline culture narratives, it is understandable why the status quo continues to prevail - high achievement for most mainstream students while minimal progress is made with many nonmainstream students.

Educators must view their jobs from a broader lens than simply teaching standards. Since students are our primary stakeholders, their needs should always be put ahead of everything else. However, it is also important to understand that many of students' needs will run counter to what is most convenient for educators and staff members. Anything outside of the scope of teaching the standards, doing assigned duties, getting school test scores up, and attending necessary meetings should not be perceived as cumbersome and become a platform for contention. More simply put, if I feel I am having to call one student's parent too much because of their continued misbehavior, it should not become a problem or a basis for complaining. If I need to spend extra time helping a student with skills because she is not at a certain readiness level, it should not become a basis for complaining, belittling the student, or belittling the student's family. For example, if an educator needs to spend additional time making accommodations so a student who constantly arrives to school late can get breakfast so she can be healthy and productive, it should not become a problem or a basis for complaining. No matter how much we as an educational community choose to complain or engage in rhetoric about them, these students will still come to our schools with the same needs. Complaining, sarcasm, and condescension towards these students, or alienating them as well as their families will not contribute to improving their achievement or meeting their needs. So, a constructive and solutions-driven mindset is necessary. Further, when we see the same outcome where the same category of students continuously achieve success, while other categories of students underachieve, yet we continue using the same approaches, we send an implicit message that the educational system and its policies cater to a targeted group of students instead of all students. Consequently, that message becomes clear to nonmainstream students and families which compels them to draw the conclusion that the educational system is only designed for a certain group of people to be successful. For this reason, the messaging behind what we say, what we do, and our approaches as well as strategies in meeting ALL students' needs is especially important if we want to obtain buy-in and inspire students to achieve.

When Lesson Plans Fail

Educators should take ownership and be willing to serve in a first responder capacity for meeting students' needs. We cannot get caught up in a blame game of who should be doing what for students. If we see students who have unmet needs and those needs are essential for their success, the buck stops with us in helping to fulfill them. It is important that we take ownership without complaining. As educators, we all need to show a willingness to give students those extras if we want to increase the likelihood of changing their outcomes as well as changing the perceptions and buy-in from their families. Our personal or societal biases should not be the cause for limiting our capacity in working with students. Complaints are most reflective of things people fail to see value in. For the most part, our biases shape our opinions around what we do or do not value, and they are usually the cause for us alienating or giving up on students. For many students, the stakes are too high for us to allow prejudicial opinions to influence our ability to meet the individual needs of students. We expect biological and stepparents to have parental instincts that compel them to make accommodations for meeting the needs of their children. If we stand "in loco parentis" (in place of the parent) when students come to schools, parents and guardians have the right to expect these same instincts from us when students are in our care. I have heard educators say, "If I had that kid for a week in my house, he would be straightened out." While we may not have legal parental rights over a child, it is essential we intrinsically embrace them as though we do and value meeting the needs of each child as they were our own. I believe all educators possess the intention of doing their jobs effectively and positively influencing students' lives. Sending a message which supports students in positive change and influence requires us to show it in our thoughts and actions just as much as in our words and slogans.

Resource for Improving Messaging – Quality Evaluation Systems

Standardized test scores should not be a stand-alone indicator for schools and districts evaluating messaging and overall effectiveness. Solely relying on test scores perpetuates a standards and metrics driven culture. Further, academic or behavioral initiatives and programs should not exist in our schools for showcase if they are not yielding meaningful results. Programs, protocol, and policy within educational communities should address the goal and purpose of why they were created. However, if messaging is unclear to the stakeholders (students, parents, staff, etc.) who participate in these initiatives and programs, it will likely hinder achieving the intended goal or purpose. Implementing quality evaluations will provide relevant and meaningful feedback for determining messaging. Additionally, quality evaluations will assist program leaders and facilitators in determining the things that are effective and should remain in place as well as the things that are ineffective and need to change.

Educational communities should have a well thought out resource for assessing the effectiveness of ALL programs and initiatives relative to their impact of specific messaging and performance in their educational setting. To promote a student-centered culture, educational communities should incorporate evaluation systems that ensure all programs and initiatives reflect a high level of expectation for student improvement. Even in programs where there are low percentages of student involvement, it is essential to incorporate thoughtful and consistent stakeholder evaluations to ensure achievement and productive messaging are occurring. Additionally, quality evaluation systems create cultures where all stakeholders are aware of the importance of reflecting upon as well as assessing approaches and strategies in pursuit of better outcomes. If the educational communities expect students and families to reflect upon and evaluate their ways of doing things, it is essential for educational communities to model the same exercise.

Organizational evaluations should engage as broad a sample of participants as possible. This does not necessarily mean everyone should or will participate, but it is important to have an adequate sample from each participant group. In the case of an after-school program, for example, be sure to have an adequate sample of teachers, caregivers, program assistants, students, parents, volunteers, and any other represented groups who are involved in the program. Involving a broad sample of participants in the evaluation process will produce rich data that comes from a variety of perspectives, and it also gives all participants an equity stake. If the data you receive is viewed from an objective lens, it should give diverse insights relative to what is working well, what needs to improve, or what needs to be discontinued. Further, by simply involving participants in the evaluation process, you are likely to find people who are willing to take a more active role of involvement – something you may not have found out if they had not participated in the evaluation. There are many parents and community stakeholders who do not assertively ask to be involved, but they will get involved if the right opportunity presents itself.

Whatever style of evaluation districts and schools choose, it should address a few things. First, it should allow stakeholders the opportunity to make open comments for each evaluation item. While Likert Scale and numeric evaluations may be convenient, it is hard to gauge the scope of opinions based solely on numbers or "Agree," "Don't Know" or "Disagree." Giving stakeholders the opportunity for open commentary provides better insight on what a 2 out of 5 rating means as numeric ratings can potentially have a broad continuum relative to meaning. Essentially, stakeholder comments on the evaluation will eliminate some of the guesswork. Second, the evaluation should attempt to gauge the participants' opinions and feelings about what is being evaluated. Some may disagree about involving stakeholder feelings in the evaluation process, but people's feelings play a significant role in shaping their opinions. Evaluations that gauge participant feelings allow for a platform of greater transparency, and they also provide a snapshot of what is needed to increase the common ground between the district, school, and stakeholders. Third, evaluations should allow stakeholders the opportunity to express what they believe is working well, what needs improving, or what needs to be changed. This can provide useful information as it relates to the depth of stakeholder engagement. For example, if a stakeholder evaluation speaks to intricate components such as improving time management or increasing the rigor of content, that would be more detailed and substantive feedback from a stakeholder than if they were to make a general statement such as, "The adults are not helping my child." In either case, however, it does provide data for assisting districts and schools with personalizing their stakeholder interactions. However, districts and schools should be willing to pay attention and actively respond to the data.

"The Activity and Program Evaluation" on page 48 can be a helpful administrative or teacher resource in evaluating initiatives within district and school settings. As discussed previously, quality evaluations should gather feedback from as broad a sample of stakeholders as possible to ensure multiple stakeholder groups have the ability to assess the program, activity, or initiative. However, it is also essential that leaders, staff members, or the stakeholders designated to spearhead the evaluation process ensure the evaluations assess the effectiveness of specific criteria to ensure they are adequately represented in the programs and initiatives. First, the evaluated program should be inserted in the oval at the top of this evaluation tool. This is the easy part because districts and schools often have a variety of programs and activities in place, and they should be easily identifiable. However, the next steps in the process become a little more engaging and will probably require deeper consideration and discussion.

There should be a tool and method for assessing ALL programs and activities utilized within an educational setting. When a teacher does a lesson on fractions, her formative and summative assessments provide her with the data to determine whether the lesson is effective and reaching the students. This way, she can make instructional decisions for better meeting the needs of students. The programs and activities within the educational setting should be looked at in the same way. If there is not a consistent assessment tool being used to determine the effectiveness of the program, activity, or initiative, how can you ensure its effectiveness? Thus, the method of assessment should be identified in the rectangular box in this evaluation tool. If you discover the program or activity being evaluated does not have a consistent assessment or a method of assessment (i.e. assessment tool, frequency, etc.), your first step is to identify an effective assessment tool for the specific program or activity. Identifying and implementing the right type of assessment should involve a high level of collegial discussion, and it should not be a cookie-cutter approach. The same assessment cannot be used for every program and activity in a district or school because all programs are different, and they have different goals as well as intentions. So, the appropriate assessment tool needs to be in place for each program or activity because it will ensure that there is a reflective process involved for measuring program effectiveness.

Programs and activities in educational communities should not be created or organized with unilateral intentions. To meet the diverse needs of learners, the programs, activities, and initiatives erected in educational communities should be multifaceted and diverse in participation as well as in contribution. The last part of the Activity and Program Evaluation gives stakeholders the opportunity to assess the volume of feedback and contribution that comes from three sources – school, home, and social capital. If an evaluator cannot list any social capital resources (i.e. guest speakers, influential community leaders, etc.) for the program or activity, that would mean more consideration should be given to involve this facet into the program or activity being evaluated.

Activity and Program Evaluation

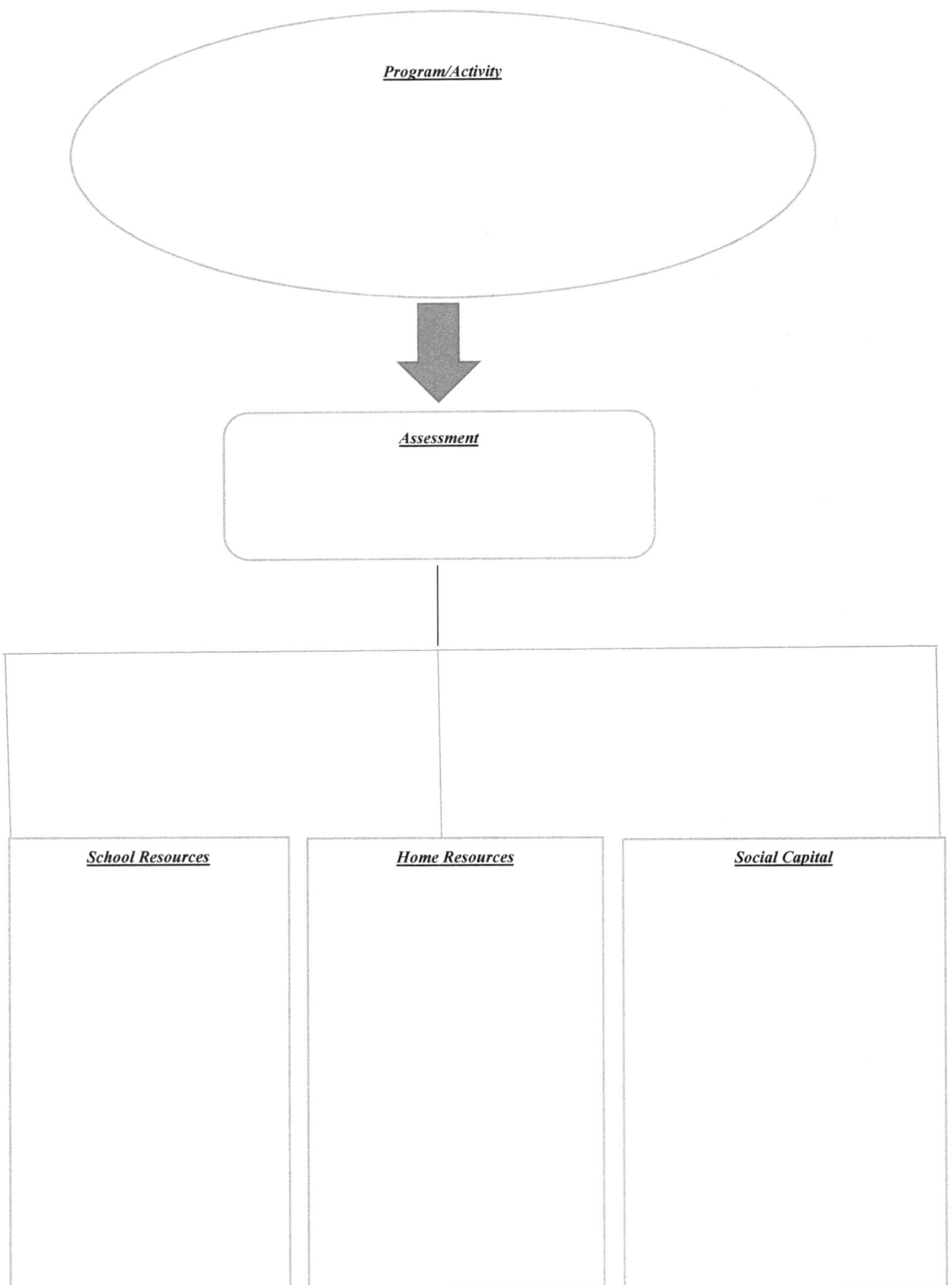

Do Not Just Go Through the Motions

Evaluations can be administered as surveys, interviews, focus groups or any other method that has proven effective within the district or school culture. However, the evaluations cannot just be in place for the sake of checking them off the "to do" list. Additionally, an evaluation should not be chosen out of convenience or because it is what has always been done. It is important that your program and activity evaluations provide meaningful data and feedback that will assist with decision-making as well as follow through. An educational community should have consistent evaluations in place that intentionally reflect on ALL their programs and activities. This reflective process should help with validating effectiveness because if the same students are underperforming or there are adversely impacted frequent flyers within those programs or activities, it is obviously ineffective to continue using the same approach in the same way for those students it intends to serve. As an educational community, we send a contradicting message when we say we want what is best for students as it relates to their success yet continue utilizing unsuccessful approaches with the expectation of a different outcome. Continuous evaluation and reasonable modifications are expected with academic instruction, curriculum, and standards. Therefore, the same things should be implemented to monitor the effectiveness for behavioral programs and other initiatives and systems that are associated with overall student development in schooling.

Points of Reflection

Consistent messaging should begin at the district and school level and permeate through to each classroom as well as in our dealings with each individual student and family. Because schools, teachers, and staff are on the front lines of education, it is essential the messaging to students and relevant stakeholders is that of being student focused. Everything we say and do as educators should be for the purpose of growing, developing, and improving students. The programs and initiatives within an educational setting should holistically compliment the goals and purposes of the organization. If districts and schools are not proactive with using quality evaluation tools that meaningfully reflect upon the programs, policies, and activities within their organizations, it increases the likelihood of there being certain students or groups of students who continuously underperform or who are subsequently marginalized because their specific needs go unidentified or unaddressed. Quality evaluations will help ensure the words and actions of educators or the programs and initiatives within an educational setting send a clear message of maximizing student achievement through collaboration, reflection, and modification. If there is not positive and consistent messaging in school settings through actions as well as words, it will ultimately perpetuate a cycle of disconnect between educators and many students as well as their families.

Achieving optimal messaging requires compromise and evaluation. Sending a constructive message to students and families may require withholding judgement in addition to being inconvenienced at times, but it will inspire the growth of students and contribute to building successful collaborative partnerships in the longer term. As educators, if improving student growth and achievement are our goals, we should be willing to assess ALL our practices and make the necessary changes to maximize the potential of achieving these goals. The goal to grow and improve students should not be more lip service than actionable service.

Chapter 3

Confronting Bias

This is the most important section of the book because mostly every rule, protocol, or system within our society is influenced by this concept. In today's polarized society, bias is often not thought of in a healthy or positive context. Some might unconsciously associate one's admission of bias to them also being a bigot, racist, misogynist, etc. While bias is a catalyst for the previously mentioned divisive terms, being biased is also a part of being human. Bias is a natural part of most normal lifestyles because by our human nature, we have favorites, preferences, and prejudices. However, if there is a lack of awareness of how our biases influence our interactions relative to the context of our jobs, it can lead to imbalance and inequity within school cultures that is detrimental to many students and their achievement.

The Influence of Bias on Decisions

Practically everyone has a preference of where they like to eat when they go out. For example, if you are confronted with a group decision between going to your favorite restaurant versus going to one that is not your personal favorite you will undoubtedly be biased towards choosing your place of preference. If someone in the group prefers another restaurant and challenges your choice, the first thing you will more than likely do is highlight the positives of your favorite restaurant while highlighting the deficiencies of the other one. Whether it be politics, favorite sports teams, favorite cars, etc. our human tendency is to speak highly of things or ideas we favor while unconsciously lessening the thing that we do not favor. So, it is human nature to have bias toward one thing over another.

While being biased toward football teams, restaurants, or a certain model of car is human nature and is embedded within the genetic code of human society, we should be mindful to limit the allowance of too much bias into district, school and classroom settings. Thus, it is important for educators to know and understand the biases they bring with them into classrooms because students are people rather than products or services. It is equally important that educators understand how the influences of historic organizational and systemic biases impact their assumptions and perceptions when interacting with students and families. Allowing personal biases and the influences of systemic biases to objectify students and families will hinder the ability to build meaningful relationships, thus hindering student progress in the areas of socioemotional and academic development.

If you were to spend time thinking critically about the historical development of our financial, criminal justice, and education policy frameworks, they have all been organized and structured around a premise of bias. As it relates to the financial system, society automatically frames a person as wealthy if they are famous, make a considerable amount of money, have substantial money in the stock market, own a lot of property, own a well-known business, or even if someone is debt free. However, if someone falls into categories outside of these, they are more than likely considered an "Ordinary Joe" relative to their wealth and finances. Similarly, in the criminal justice system, if someone has an offense on their record, it becomes a challenge for him or her to obtain gainful employment. The offense may have been years ago, but the legal system has instilled a bias within societal code that if an individual has had anything other than a minor run-in with the law, a prospective employer should think twice before hiring that person for a job or, in certain instances, even allowing him to vote. Further, if a child's parents or relatives have been in and out of jail, bias will often influence people's perceptions of that child because they will often conclude the child is destined for the same path as their relatives. So, bias is the cause of many students being stereotyped and stigmatized before adequate time is invested in getting to know them as the unique individuals they are.

In many circumstances, lawyers use reputation, characteristics, and previous infractions against someone who is on trial because they know it has the potential to provoke the bias of a jury in concluding whether the accused is innocent or guilty of a certain offense. In some instances, this approach sways jurors' perceptions of innocence or guilt prior to all the facts and evidence being presented. Similarly, intentional and unintentional bias within the educational community plays a role in formulating perceptions of what a successful or unsuccessful student should look like in our schools. If a student is on the honor roll, does not openly challenge the teacher or rules, is always on time to school or class, and does not have to spend time in ISS or OSS, etc. she is considered the cream of the crop within the student population – a high achieving mainstream student. If this type of student ever has a behavior infraction, she is seen as a work in progress who is going to make mistakes sometimes. On the other hand, students who have been to ISS or OSS struggle with following rules or are not on the honor roll are seen as not working up to their potential, unconcerned about their future, or about being a better student. At times, bias manifests into formulating perceptions about the student's family. For example, if a student were to commit an offense that causes them to get a referral and a school representative attempts to call the parent two or three times, bias (in some cases) has influenced the school representative's perception and has led him or her to draw the conclusion that the parent is uninvolved or unconcerned about the student's struggles at school. Subsequently, the bias embedded within our systems and organizational cultures can automatically and unconsciously connect many of our perceptions to negative or positive attributes without having knowledge of or understanding the full story. Unless we learn to acknowledge and neutralize the preexisting biases within our personal lives as well as in the current systems and structures, we, as educators, will alienate many students and their families. This will prevent us from making significant progress in narrowing the home-school disconnect and the overall achievement gap.

Understanding the Degrees of Bias

Much of the initial discourse about bias usually centers around explicit or implicit. However, it is important to investigate the influences bias has on thinking in addition to the implications as it relates to decisions, strategies, and protocol. In my opinion, while this discussion is important to be held at a broader societal context, it is of the utmost priority to have this discussion more immediately in P-12 education. The degrees of bias discussed here are intended to be an extension to Estella Bensimon's (2005) work pertaining to the cognitive frames. In her research, Bensimon identifies three levels of cognitive frames: deficit, diversity, and equity. Her research provokes discussion and consideration for how bias relative to organizational and institutional thinking potentially create educational settings where student needs are neglected due to a lack of equity and access. It is important to expand upon Bensimon's work for two main reasons. First, Bensimon's (2005) work mostly focuses on how the cognitive frames impact higher education settings. However, it is important to broaden this discussion to explore how the same biases in thinking influence the P-12 arena. Second, it is essential to expand on this work because it speaks to the importance of shining a light on how bias influences thinking – which subsequently impacts the action or inaction related to protocol and policy. If bias plays too much of a role in the thinking and the actions or inactions of enough people who influence policy within educational settings, it will undoubtedly influence achievement and performance of the groups of students that fall on the wrong side of the biased thinking that is associated with the actions or inactions. Ultimately, bias affects thinking, attitudes, and actions, and no students should be denied access to opportunity or resources because of these factors.

First, let me provide a disclaimer that I am not an attorney, and I do not practice law. I do not possess a Juris Doctor (JD) nor do I hold any other credential that certifies or qualifies me to practice law or render legal advice. Having stated that, I utilize examples from the legal field for the sole purpose of establishing a conceptual parallel to compare those terms often used in the legal field to better understanding what is meant by varying degrees of bias. Within the legal system, there are varying degrees of assault and murder. Cases are often heard where a prosecutor may be attempting to persuade a jury that the accused is guilty of one degree of assault or murder while the defense attorney may be attempting to persuade the jury their client is either totally innocent or guilty of a lesser degree of assault or murder. In legal terms, this is more commonly thought of as first, second, or third degrees of assault or murder.

Before delving into a description of the degrees of bias and the table, I must emphasize the importance of viewing this text from an objective lens. First, everyone will more than likely have different degrees of biases for different issues. Someone may have first-degree bias when it comes to their beliefs relating to smoking whereas the same person may have third-degree bias (little bias at all) as it pertains to their beliefs about drinking. So, it is the issue or idea that impacts the degree of bias a person has. Second, in order to maximize understanding of the degrees of bias, it is important to not get overly consumed with the scenarios being presented. So, please do not be quick to take offense to the scenarios because the degrees of bias have less to do with the situation and more to do with how bias influences attitudes and thinking, which subsequently will influence strategies and approaches. So, the intent is to provide sample illustrations of how the attitudes and thinking of biased people can potentially influence their strategies and approaches, especially with issues they feel the strongest about. Connecting this back to education, if there is an inability by educators or the educational community to diligently reflect and take an honest inventory of how our biases influence our thoughts and attitudes associated with interactions, decisions, and policy, it will further hinder us from doing what is equitable for meeting many of our students' needs.

Lastly, some may feel like it is callous or insensitive to make a correlation between the degrees of assault or murder to the degrees of bias. However, I believe it is reasonable to associate the degrees of bias in a similar context. Words and actions are often influenced by the extent or degree of bias. If we put this into further perspective, how many students' and families' ways of life, priorities, and values have been assaulted or assassinated due to bias-filled rhetoric, thinking, or decisions made by those with influence or by those who are in leadership? Since individual and systemic biases influence organizational decisions and policies relative to schooling, it is reasonable to conclude that a person or organization whose thinking is influenced by a greater degree of bias will more than likely make decisions, policy, and protocol that directly or indirectly appeals to his or her preferences, perceptions, and assumptions. While this may benefit those with access, influence, and power, it can be damaging if it occurs too frequently within a diverse culture. If bias goes unchecked, it potentially becomes a major influence of division within organizational culture. In our case, that means a significant group of students, families, and stakeholders (many who are nonmainstream) will be alienated, neglected, and in some cases, omitted. This makes it virtually impossible to foster an effective and successful learning environment for ALL.

Degrees of Bias

Degree	Looks Like	Sounds Like	Likely Stakeholder Outcome
1st	Intentional & Direct	"My belief/position is the one that is right and matters most. All other beliefs/positions are less of a priority."	Callous, insensitive interactions and intentional limitations to resources due to a lack of concern; Students/families with similar beliefs/positions will strive, but likely a high-tension cultural setting for all other students/families.
2nd	Equality/Limited Equity	"All students/families have access to the same things. They are responsible for using those resources in the most effective ways."	Privileged students/families are more likely to strive in this setting; Underachievement or inadequate results for students/families that require greater access due to situations and circumstances; Mostly a positive cultural setting for privileged students/families whereas indifferent and blame-filled cultural setting for other students/families.
3rd	Empathy/Limited Solution	"Some students/families do have greater need than others, but resources (i.e. time, funding, social capital, etc.) are limited. We are doing as much as we can with what we have."	High achievement for privileged students as well as underprivileged/marginalized students who have access to social capital; Likely underachievement or inadequate results for others; A positive cultural setting for privileged students/families and those with access to social capital. A superficial cultural setting for other students/families.

Bias in the First Degree

Bias in the first degree is intentional and direct, and it resembles Estella Bensimon's (2005) principle of the deficit cognitive frame. In sum, this is where the dominant culture blames the oppressed for their (the oppressed) own problems. Similarly, first-degree bias usually has little regard for perspectives, thoughts, and values outside of what they believe to be appropriate or true. While all the degrees of bias involve some form of intent, those with first-degree bias are more premeditated in their actions or inactions. Further, someone with first-degree bias is more likely to give the benefit of the doubt to a rule violator who has similar beliefs, but they will likely take the same violation to more of an extreme if it involves someone who does not share their common belief.

For example, a staff member who has first-degree bias when it comes to student dress code notices a student who wears his pants at his waist and is well-groomed talking loudly in the hall and chooses to reprimand him with a subtle verbal warning. However, if the same staff member sees a different student talking loudly who is wearing torn jeans and flip flops and reprimands him in a more confrontational and coercive way (i.e. interrogation, ultimatums, etc.), it is safe to conclude that the distinction between the two reprimands (all other things being equal) can be attributed to the staff member's first-degree bias associated with appearance. Both students could have been on the honor roll and in good class standing, but the staff member's first-degree bias toward how one student looked potentially influenced her approach to addressing the issue. Further, if someone with first-degree bias has knowledge of someone who stands in direct opposition to what they hold to be true, they are likely to utilize microaggression - directly or indirectly conspire and plan a way to vilify, ridicule, or expel those who they know are in opposition to their beliefs or way of thinking. For example, a staff member who continuously notices a student wearing his pants low and has a first-degree bias related to that type of style is likely to escalate tensions by getting into a power struggle altercation with the student over the dress code and the letter of the law instead of deescalating the situation by exploring more peaceful and constructive solutions through private dialogue, resolution, and, when necessary, consequence.

The person who possesses first-degree bias about a certain issue may feel that escalating a matter will further demean the person and the act by bringing further attention to it in addition to the person who engages in it. Further, the person displaying first-degree bias feels if a situation is escalated in the right way, it can bring enough attention to it so as to potentially get rid of the person (the student in most cases), which also gets rid of the problem. So, in these examples, the premeditation and intent are not with addressing the issue of low pants and appearance. Instead, they are the intentions behind the approach relative to solving the problem. People with first-degree bias feel so strongly about their position that it influences their thinking and approach to potentially escalate a smaller issue into a bigger one in hopes of getting rid of the unwanted issue, person, or problem and making things more aligned with the way they think it should be.

While the issue of wearing pants low is commonplace and probably is (in many cases) a violation of dress code, it is arguably not a serious enough issue to warrant a power struggle or any type of condescending approach. Seemingly, an unbiased approach would mean being sensitive to the student's right, their background (after all, maybe low hanging pants is all they see when not at school), and his choice to accept the established consequences that go along with violation of the dress code. I underlined 'established' because there is a difference between a student receiving the pre-established consequences for violating the dress code versus the unforeseen consequences received as a byproduct of microaggression due to a staff member's bias or animosity towards a specific person or behavior. If the above scenarios seemed rigid and extreme, it is likely that appearance or dress code is not a first-degree bias issue for you. So, while you may believe that appearance and dress code are important (You may even have a degree of bias as it relates to student appearance), it may not necessarily be your "hot button" issue. However, the challenge for you as well as all educators is to identify the issues where your most extreme first-degree bias habitates so that it does not negatively affect your ability to reasonably and equitably make decisions for respectfully interacting with students, families, and other stakeholders.

Bias in the Second Degree

Bias in the second degree resembles Bensimon's (2005) concept of diversity cognitive frame. This is where everyone has equal access to the same things; thus, the same opportunity to be successful. Bias in the second degree can be misleading because equality is most often associated with fairness, but that is not necessarily the case. I once played on a coed company softball team. There was a broad range of experience levels on the softball team. Some people had many years of softball experience while others had not even picked up a bat or a glove. I had experience playing Little League Baseball growing up, but I had never played slow pitch softball. I was accustomed to swinging the bat, wearing the glove, and all other aspects associated with baseball, but I was not skilled at how to swing at a slow pitch softball. While I was in a better position than some teammates who had no experience, it took extra time for me to learn a slow pitch softball swing instead of the fast pitch baseball swing. I spent time consulting with the softball pros of the team as well as going to Frankie's Fun Park to get some repetitions on the softball pitch machine. The point here is that everyone had equal access to the field, gloves, bats within our set practice times, but that still was not enough for many of us. Because of our experiences or lack thereof, we needed more access to those items so that we could have a better chance of performing at a high level.

People with second-degree bias may often use equal access as a scapegoat. They feel that if everyone is getting equal, no one can make a viable excuse for an inability to excel or achieve. People with second-degree bias may take exception to the notion of having to provide more to one person than another because in their minds, they feel it is not right for one person to get more than another. Connecting this to education, some educators believe that because every student has equal access to the instructional content, the textbook, chrome book, as well as to the teacher, there is no excuse why a student should not be able to do the work. However, in considering the softball story, how reasonable would that expectation be? In a class there are different students coming from different household structures with different background knowledge in addition to having different perceptions of school. It would be unreasonable to think that all students can achieve at the same level simply because they have equal access to materials and resources. Additionally, the age and experiences of the students will play a factor. Equitable time as well as resources will have to be invested in many students in order to get them achieving at the same high level as others, especially if the expectation is to get them to perform at the same level as those students who have more frequent access to quality resources outside of the school setting.

Bias in the Third Degree

Third degree-bias is less polarizing, intentional, and oppositional than first and second-degree bias. Bias in the third degree resembles Bensimon's (2005) equity cognitive frame. This is where organizations consider their deficiencies instead of finding a way to blame those who are marginalized (i.e. students and families). While third-degree bias is more empathetic towards student needs in correlation to resources (or lack thereof), it is still important to address the thoughts and approaches associated with this type of bias because they could have the potential to negatively impact growth and achievement if not carefully scrutinized. In my opinion, third-degree bias is the category where a legitimate number of districts, schools, and staff fall into for a legitimate number of issues relative to interaction, protocol, and achievement. If we are honest about it, there are a surplus of student and family needs existing in many educational communities but usually not a surplus of critical resources required to meet those needs. Unfortunately, that has become an accepted reality in education, but we still should remember that we are tasked with producing high-achieving students. Additionally, while third-degree bias is the lowest degree of bias, it still involves bias. So, it is important to understand how thinking and approaches are influenced in this category.

An educator who teaches, mentors, or counsels transient, high poverty, and underprivileged nonmainstream students may know that his students have significant socioemotional and academic needs. Additionally, the educator may know that available school-based resources are not adequate to meet the needs of many of his students. While that may be the reality in many cases, educators should be mindful not to allow this to distort their beliefs, thinking, and their approaches. It can be especially easy to fall into third-degree bias when teaching and serving students who have encountered issues such as violence, abuse, and other childhood traumas.

For example, students whose parents are incarcerated and have a history of crime and violence in their family will likely be more immediately blamed and scrutinized by a first or second-degree bias teacher. However, teachers with third-degree bias will likely give more compassion and consideration to these students as it relates to their outside-of-school issues. Third-degree bias teachers are more likely to invest the time to become familiar with students' background and will acknowledge the fact that these students have a variety of crucial basic (Maslow's) needs that have been neglected. While these teachers are aware of these factors, they also know that mental health counseling in the school setting is limited, and the school counselor can only schedule minimal weekly sessions with the student. So, they recommend these students for the services. In many instances, after school programs may be the only other school-based alternatives for students. So, the teachers also recommend these students for those services as well. However, if the teacher stops there with pursuing additional resources, this would be an example of third-degree bias. This teacher is aware his students have needs that go above and beyond the scope of traditional school resources, but only goes as far as the standardized, school-based resources (i.e. counseling schedule, after school programs, etc.) to meet those students' needs. While the teacher does take the time to explore the mainstream alternatives the school offers to help this student, he still knows the student's needs require more resources. It is true that this teacher would be displaying more empathy and compassion for these students than a first or second-degree bias teacher. However, while the third-degree bias teachers are more considerate of those students' needs, if they know that these resources are not enough, but stops any way once they have explored the standardized and mainstream options, it would be an example of third-degree bias. Similarly, some educators may feel that because they have explored these and other outside of the classroom options for these types of students that it is enough. At this point, it becomes easier to blame home, the family or the student because these educators feel they have the right do so in consideration of their extra efforts.

The Powerless Power Struggles

A deeper investigation into the degrees of bias should help in gaining better understanding of why blame games and power struggles exist within the educational community. Arguably, our biases and the thinking, attitudes, and perceptions associated with them cause many of the power struggles and polarizations existing within districts, schools, classrooms, and society. It is essential for educators and educational communities to be cognizant of situations and circumstances where bias contributes to the escalation instead of de-escalation of issues because unnecessary power struggles are counterproductive in building positive and engaging educational communities. All educators will encounter power struggles with students and parents, but the outcome will be contingent upon how reasonably these struggles can be resolved. Undoubtedly, it is essential for administrators to be in control of their schools and for teachers to be in control of their classrooms. However, being in control does not necessarily equate to having to be authoritative or controlling.

In a household, for example, it is not necessary for parents to exercise some sort of controlling dominance over their children to show they are in charge. The parent can be the authority without always using coercive authoritative devices (i.e. yelling, threats, ultimatums, coercions, or condescending overtures). The fact that a parent pays the rent or mortgage, supplies children with food, clothing, as well as a sense of well-being and normalcy (which of course varies from household to household) somewhat preestablishes them as having authority. However, most parents probably also know that kids will be kids, and they will at some point do something that is contrary to what is expected. Does a parent being condescending help change the behavior of their child in this situation? From my personal experiences as a parent (also a stepparent for some years), I can say when I tried this approach, the children still frequently repeated the behaviors that I was trying to deter them from doing either to show me my strategy was ineffective or simply because they were children. And we know that children usually have to bump their heads multiple times to develop a better understanding of how to handle something in a different way. Additionally, my parenting experiences revealed that yelling, threats, ultimatums, coercion, and condescension usually did little to diminish unwanted behaviors. I always seemed to have to repeatedly address the behavior as well as assign new consequences. So, the point is that as powerful as I tried to make myself appear by raising my voice, using condescending undertones (i.e. "I thought you were intelligent enough to know not do something as immature as this!"), or using threats and ultimatums, it really proved how powerless I was when it came to changing my own children's behaviors. The truth is that while our approaches may play a role in changing kids' behaviors, a majority of the decision will be contingent on the child and her motivation to change. If that is the case, it seems that taking a collaborative and team-centered approach would motivate children to move in that direction before a confrontational approach would. Another important lesson parenting has taught me is that those actions on my part only stopped my children or a student from doing the behavior one time, but it did not establish a constructive framework for deterring them from ever doing the behavior again. So, my coercive approaches only impacted behaviors for the short term, which does not translate into helping develop lifelong skills. Ultimately, there is no power and authority in that.

As educators, we should adopt the notion of valuing the communication and interaction with all the students we serve at schools just as much as we value it with our own biological or stepchildren. None of us can pretend that our biological children or stepchildren are perfect, and they always got it right the first time they were told to do something. For those who have raised multiple children, we also understand that development is different between each child. Your first child may have developed an understanding, mastery, or compliance to something quicker than your second child. So, while some approaches may be similar between your children, you sometimes have to modify them to a degree because of the differences that exist between children. Similarly, it should be understood that students will bring different family values and priorities to school with them.

Responsible adults and educators owe students more than just teaching them standards and holding them accountable for following protocol. In addition, we should be willing to nurture and show students how to properly behave during times of challenges, confusions, frustrations, and even in confrontations because it's those situations where students are looking and listening in the most intent way. If we handle those situations in an irresponsible way (i.e. yelling, condescension, coercion, threats, ultimatums, etc.), we consequently authorize students to do the same because children learn an abundance of their behaviors from…**adults**. If we as educators overcompensate in modeling the use of controlling type behaviors and approaches, students will consequently mimic us when they encounter challenges. The irony is that the same educators who choose to display these types of approaches are likely to be the recipients of those same approaches, courtesy of the students who have witnessed those educators in action. So, for any educator who labels students as uncaring, apathetic, and unwilling; suggesting they have no family values or structure, are thugs, etc., please be mindful to reflect upon how the behaviors students see and hear from you may correlate with the label you are assigning to them.

Before the authoritative and 'no non-sense' educators write this off as foolish and ineffective rhetoric, I am not suggesting that establishing rules and consequences are not necessary because they absolutely are. Additionally, there are instances where students should know firm expectations as well as accountability. Whether it be our own children or our students, they must understand there are expectations and boundaries. However, what I am calling into question here are the quality of certain strategies and approaches we choose as well as the intention behind using them. The fact is that if yelling, condescension, coerciveness, and threats are the dominant strategies in our educational settings with respect to how we interact with students and families, we cannot honestly say that we're concerned about meeting the holistic needs of students and their families. Zealously adopting the use of these approaches becomes more about our bias and our power assertion under the pretense of getting students to follow and comply with rules or simply to get rid of them. In either case, these strategies lend themselves to a standards-based approach rather than on constructively developing students through a stakeholder engagement approach. If our goal is to bring out the best in the students and families we serve relative to character development and academic achievement, yelling, condescension, coercions, threats, and ultimatums should not be our most effective and frequently used strategies in achieving these goals. Regardless of whether you are an administrator, teacher, or support staff, if you are in P-12 education, it is essential to remember that the students you serve are **children,** and they need to be afforded latitude to err and make corrections at different rates and levels. If we do not remember this at the classroom and the school level, bias will cause us to misuse or overuse unproductive strategies that will prove ineffective for growing students.

Certainly, a child's urgency to correct behaviors is influenced by their cognitive ability, but it is also influenced by their experiences, their socioemotional development, and the degree to which their basic needs have been met. All three of these factors are heavily influenced by their home life and upbringing, things over which educators do not have control. So, if we, as educators, embrace the ideologies of yelling, belittling, or threatening our way into making students comply, research shows these approaches are unrealistic and unproven. Ultimately, these approaches will not help build rapport with students, bring out the best in them, or generate family support.

A further truth is there are some in our profession who choose not to monitor and adjust their behaviors and will rely on the same tactics without considering how those approaches impact students' growth and achievement. I contend that educators who remain in this place do so because it is easier and more convenient. It is easier for these educators to assign blame to how bad today's children and families are instead of evaluating and modifying their interactional approaches, which is especially important for nonmainstream students. It is also probable they do this because it is more important to get students to comply to the standard protocol than it is for them to be attentive in meeting the specific needs of the child. Adopting this rationale is a contributing factor to why many nonmainstream students and their families lack trust in our schools, disengage, and ultimately check out because it is moments like the above example where they realize that educators' priorities are on standards and protocol rather than on meeting their needs.

Just because threats or condescending tones give the appearance of keeping things quiet and orderly does not mean the best is being brought out in students. Evidence suggests that one of the primary elements of achievement is creativity. Evidence also suggests that a predominantly authoritative classroom suppresses student creativity because students are often fearful of stepping outside of the teachers' established boundaries. Consequently, certain students will underperform in this type of classroom setting because their creative selves are not fully engaged. On the contrary, evidence also suggests there are disadvantages to the overly relaxed classroom too because students are not held accountable for much and consequently, too much of their efforts are devoted to irrelevant or underdeveloped tasks that do not hold them accountable for high achievement. Essentially, striking a balanced, stakeholder engagement-driven approach is critical to developing a meaningful learning culture.

If the goal is to keep our students in a head space that is conducive to learning, self-regulation, and self-empowerment, wouldn't it be more favorable to actively explore ways of granting them access to the school resources they're seeking instead of engaging in a power struggle - which will more than likely disengage them from feeling a sense of self-regulation or self-empowerment? Why does it feel like the focus of many of our educational settings has become more about trying to catch those students and families we presume are attempting to get away with things, beat the system and our desire to put them in their place? Should that be the purpose behind what we do in our educational system, trying to keep our feet on the necks of the presumed slackers at the expense of denying those who are crying out for us to help meet their needs?

To frame this discourse as allowing students and families to get their way is unrealistic and hypocritical because if many of us are honest with ourselves, somewhere in our past (or present) we acquired a free pass or we gained access to something we did not do the most diligent work to earn. Has any adult reading this book ever received a warning ticket as opposed to the actual speeding ticket you deserved? Better yet, has any educator gotten a pass for turning lesson plans in late, showing up late for duty, or leaving students unsupervised? Yet, some students are often judged and denied equitable access to beneficial resources because they fall prey to someone who has the biased perception that most students and their families are attempting to game the system. In too many instances, it seems that the intention of some educators is to be tight on the rules so the ones attempting to play the system do not get a free pass. However, in relentlessly tightening the rules, they also deprive and limit access to students who the resources were designed to benefit in the first place. Our perceptions and assumptions of what should be most important to students are not always what is true, and it is imperative that we accept that reality. If students' needs are not first, they are last, and our standards-driven approaches and biases frequently prevent students and families from feeling their needs come first. If students and their families perceive this to be the case, we, as educators, will struggle with getting the highest level of performance from students along with the degree of meaningful support we seek from home.

Will Bias or Benevolence Prevail?

I recall working extensively with four siblings in a school. The youngest was in third grade, two were in fifth grade, and one was in eighth grade. The fifth and eighth grade siblings encountered frequent discipline issues throughout the school year. School protocol required teachers to communicate with parents when there were discipline concerns. However, teachers often complained about not being able to contact the parents when issues arose. The teachers for the eighth-grade student began expressing more frequent concerns about him being silly and disengaged during class. A couple of them said when they attempted to reach the parent, the student would answer the phone and say she was unavailable. I began to mentor him and check on his progress more frequently. Rather than punish the student for each infraction, I attempted to intervene by allowing him to sit in my office space to complete his work and have discussions with him about different courses of action. Some teachers did not agree with this approach because they felt that his not being held accountable each time would send the wrong message to other students. I had already communicated with the parent about other sibling behavioral issues earlier in the year, and I also experienced some challenges with reaching her. However, she always seemed supportive when we communicated. So, I called to speak with her about these concerns.

During this conversation, the mother revealed she had recently gone through a divorce, and the other parent, who was also the major bread winner, left the family. Consequently, this forced her to have to move into a smaller home and find more work to support the family. She also explained that she worked frequently throughout the day, and she often worked into the night hours, which placed a lot of responsibility on the older siblings because she could not afford a sitter. I collaborated with the school counselor, and we conducted a home visit. During this visit, we discovered she also had two more infant children. They lived in a home with a kitchen, a living room, and only one bedroom of operable living space. Most of the older kids slept in the living room because they had no rooms of their own. The parent experienced numerous mechanical problems with her vehicle, and it was evident the temporary license tag had been on the car for an extended period. Because of problems with the vehicle, there were times the parent had to arrange for transportation to and from work. Additionally, the number of siblings as well as the fact that there was no washer and dryer in the home created challenges for cleaning their clothes. Going to the laundromat was expensive and often challenging due to the transportation issues and the parent's work schedule.

We began reaching out to school partners in hopes of assisting this parent with food, and rental assistance, in addition to laundering supplies. We collected clothes, blankets, and towels to give the parent and checked in weekly. We attempted to provide progress reports and teacher feedback each time we spoke. I also had a heart-to-heart talk with the older siblings to emphasize the importance of helping with chores and being obedient. For the most part, the siblings' behaviors improved, and the lines of positive communication increased between home and school.

Subsequently, this home visit gave us a better understanding of why the older school-aged siblings were experiencing some of their problems at school. It was evident the oldest child, the eighth grader, was somewhat embarrassed about this situation, which is why he was evasive about us making contact or even doing the initial home visit. It was also apparent that his recent silliness and unconcern at school were somewhat resulting from him having to be an adult at home. At home, he had adult responsibilities and school was his only retreat for being a kid. The first thing I felt compelled to do was have a conversation with his teachers and inform them of his family's situation. While the intent was not to excuse him of behavioral infractions, I asked the teachers to involve me or the counselor if the behaviors seemed to be escalating so that we could intervene before anything spiraled out of control. Needless to say, the timing of our involvement did not always correspond with bell schedules or other pre-established schedule-related protocols.

Narratives such as these speak to the importance of looking beyond the academic standards, schedules, and even the standards of behavior policy so students' needs are met. There are countless students and families with a similar scenario in quite a few schools today. However, many of them fall through the cracks because there is often the choice to focus on meeting standards and bureaucratic protocol instead of the choice to meet students' needs. Too often, educators tend to alienate or give up on students like these in our schools by placing a greater emphasis on standardized lessons and enforcing rigid behavior policy than on meeting their other needs, which often contributes to their academic or behavioral deficiencies. If the emphasis is primarily on teaching children standards and assigning consequences framed within rigid protocol and policy, the siblings discussed in this narrative would have continued a downward spiral relative to their academic and behavioral performance. Had we chosen to inundate the parent with constant bad news and undertones suggesting she and her children were inadequate (when she already had a full plate), the parent would have been less likely to engage in positive discourse and support us in our efforts at the school.

Unfortunately, the systemic bias existing within educational policy guides many of the protocols, expectations, and perceptions in schools today. However, as educators, we should ensure that our students and parents see a greater priority in us than the narrow scope of teaching standards-based lessons, providing consequences for rule breakers, and passing judgement on any students and parents who do not fall into the bias-filled norms. While learning rules and expectations is a vital part of socioemotional and academic growth, it is important we teach them in a meaningful context. Imitating the same type of bias that exists in our personal experiences as well as in our broader institutional structures will almost certainly lead to classrooms and school environments of favoritism, sarcasm, condescension, distrust, and ultimately underachievement. Arguably, the allowance of too much bias in our classroom and school settings has contributed to the high degree of contention that exists between many non-white families of nonmainstream students and the mostly White middle class teacher constituency. Further, these are many of the same students who are identified as the underperformers. Thus, beating them further into the ground with coercive approaches and corrective overtures will not magically shift their willingness to perform better.

Imagine the type of discourse that is initiated when teachers comprised of a White middle class schooling structure communicate with mostly minority nonmainstream student families – with communication that is mostly suggestive of their child's inadequacy as it relates to the way they dress, wear their hair, how they speak, how they respond to adults at school, and in their level of academic achievement within the classroom and school. What does that type of conversation look like? Does it promote collaboration, or does it promote a sense of implying that one side is better or more knowledgeable than another? Does it build a sense of agency, efficacy, or collective efficacy relative to building a partnership for the child's success, or contrarily, does it put parents on the defensive where they feel more inclined to immediately gravitate to their biases – which often include parents telling the school everything that is wrong with their teachers, their culture, their organization, and their overall structure?

The scary part is that this biased conversational battle has been ongoing for lengthy periods of time in many districts, schools, and classrooms. It has been going on for so long that much of the educational community now has changed its strategy. The new strategy is to make the first call or communication positive. The thought behind this is that if the first call is positive rather than negative, the parents will be more receptive to answering the phone and having a conversation when it is time to engage in improvement related conversations. While initiating and establishing positive dialogue are definitely essential in creating a meaningful and respectful culture, the stain of distrust created by the pre-existing discourse makes the parent immediately revert to a position of self-defense rather than a position of seeking constructive solutions. Unfortunately, no overnight solution will fix this challenge because it is deeply rooted within our educational system and blaming parents for their defensive posture or the parents who are apathetic will further contribute to what generated the problem in the first place. The best thing for us to do as an educational community is to get a grip on the cause of this communication disconnect within our schools, which often begins and ends with the presence of bias. Thus, students and parents should see and hear a transitional shift in our actions and dialogue – a shift that focuses less on what their child needs to do to align themselves with the standards of academics and behavior - and more on what we, the stakeholders, can do to help meet this child where she is so that she is more equipped to master the standards around what is expected. It is evident the standards first approach is not improving the home-school disconnect or closing the achievement gap. So, hopefully, a broad shift to the stakeholder or student needs first approach will contribute to shifting the paradigm.

Teacher Bail Outs Lead to Student Check Out

Some educators unconsciously abandon students to satisfy the status quos of school protocol, the pacing guide, and other criteria established by the bias-filled system. When this occurs, it gives the impression that the needs of the system are ahead of the needs of the student. Unfortunately, this often occurs with the students who need these educators and the extra support the most. The disappointing part is that some educators bail on students for the sake of maintaining the standards of routine (the process) and overlook the importance of shaping the product (the whole student). It is also disappointing because when an educator chooses to bail on a student to appease bureaucratic systems, they are forgetting it is these same types of systems that bail on us (educators) by using the limited data such as test scores to suggest we are not doing enough. It is imperative that educators stop abandoning students in their time of need due to drawing the conclusion that their academic progress is too low, they are taking too long to change a behavior, or their life circumstances are too complex for them (educators) to invest their time in helping the student. Truthfully, a significant number of challenges students face today (homelessness, abandonment, abuse, etc.) are beyond their direct control to fix.

Bailing on students starts when we as educators allocate time speaking condescendingly about them or their situations instead of allocating that same time helping them to find constructive solutions that can help. One indication of this is when students are intentionally denied access to resources and systems that are available to potentially assist with providing them more quality care. For example, if a student has developed a reputation for being a "drama king" and wanting to see the counselor all the time, some educators may conclude that this student's access to the counselor needs to be limited or restricted because he is going too much. So, when the student asks to see the counselor, he is not taken seriously, he is told he can't go, or he is told (sometimes in a snide or condescending way) that everything should not warrant him having to run to see the counselor. Some might look at this example and find nothing wrong, but it creates more peril if we as an educational community allow our perceptions, which are shaped and influenced by our biases, of students' current reputations to be the primary determinant for granting them access to vital school resources such as the counselor. What if this is the day that student decides that he is going to bring a gun to school the following day? What if this is the day that she decides to end it all by attempting suicide? On the other hand, what if this is the day he saw something on the chrome book about building cars and needs constructive incite from a counselor about how to harness and refine that interest into a potential career?

Unfortunately, a significant number of students who fall into this category are denied or granted only limited access to counselors, or other pertinent support staff and social capital who can mentor to them because some would rather choose to draw bias-filled conclusions about the student's motive. In doing so, these educators are choosing to bail on students because they are prioritizing the governance of standardized rules and protocol over the prospect of potentially meeting other needs that may exist for these students. A point worth reiterating is how can we expect students to be fully engaged with achieving the standards-based instruction and protocol we're attempting to provide if we do not show an invested interest in them getting other essential needs met first? In this instance, it should be easy to understand why a student might frame this experience as the educator valuing it to be more important to criticize his action or inaction or criticize his work ethic than assist him with gaining access to the essential resource the student feels he needs. Therefore, it is important that we also place a similar priority on granting students access to the resources that may not necessarily be a part of the lesson plan or in direct compliance with the standardized rules and protocol of the status quo because those needs are often just as valuable as procedures and curriculum.

If the goal is to establish or improve a sense of priority within the student (i.e. there's a time and place to spend time with the counselor), perhaps there's a way to achieve that by coupling the student's request with him meeting a reasonable expectation of productivity relative to his academic requirements. In other words, instead of denying the student access, specify a reasonable quota of work expectation for the student to complete prior to allowing him to see the counselor. This creates a win-win scenario for both sides and establishes the foundation for healthy adult-student collaboration in the future. Flat out denying him access and suggestively demeaning his motive do more to push the student away from a positive learning experience than moving him toward it. This becomes more about asserting power than it does about giving students access to resources that will promote progress. Seemingly, in this case, the power struggle relative to process would win out over the prospect of meeting the student's authentic needs.

Resource for Evaluating Bias – Bias Reflection and Intervention Inventory

Diligent reflection requires that practitioners consider how their biases influence their decisions relative to pedagogy, protocol, and process. Frankly, educators (or people in general) who claim their bias does not influence their thinking, decisions, or lifestyles are in denial, and their denial and unwillingness to evaluate themselves can have detrimental consequences when it comes to meeting the needs of certain students and learners. Denial of bias is how or why the same educators can be in their same positions, yet student achievement results go unchanged.

Ultimately, the same students or groups of students continue to underperform because the same people sitting in district offices, schools, classrooms, and board seats are unwilling to deeply investigate how their biases place a stronghold of influence on policy, protocol, and pedagogy that should be intended to help the achievement of ALL students. Consequently, the same groups of students achieve while the others continuously underachieve.

The "Bias Reflection and Intervention Inventory" is an essential tool for districts, schools, grade level teams, and individual educators to use because it requires taking an inventory of the beliefs and convictions that have the greatest potential for influencing their decision making. As stated in the degrees of bias discussion, everyone has bias, but everyone's degree of bias is different about different things. Therefore, it is important for educators to take an honest inventory of their biases, especially of things that have the potential to most directly influence their thinking and decisions when it comes to their interactions with students and families.

For educators to effectively use the inventory, it requires them to consider the beliefs and convictions they feel the strongest about because these are the most probable sources for the strongest degrees of bias. A second source of consideration would be to use common themes that exist within the demographic of students being served. For example, a teacher may hear a conversation between several students in her class about playing video games during the school week. However, the teacher may have a strong belief against children playing video games during the school week. So, in this situation, the idea that potentially sparks teacher bias would be students being allowed to play video games during the school week. This may also cause the teacher to immediately begin scrutinizing or drawing unfair conclusions about why the students who are not top performers in her classroom are being allowed to play video games. Once an educator has identified the belief or conviction, she should consider the degree of bias she has about this principle using the "Bias Reflection & Intervention" table on page 79. The next step is to consider logical reasons why or how someone might think differently about the listed principle. This part intends to provoke an educator to think outside of her feelings and consider other potential perspectives. Lastly, the educator should explore potential approaches that will allow her to become less polarized about the bias and consider compromise initiatives, especially for those things that will most directly impact classroom as well as general interactions with students and families.

If a patient were to visit his primary care doctor about a knee injury, his primary care physician may not have the experience or know how to assist the patient with his knee. However, if it is a good doctor, she will admit that knees are not her strong suit and refer the patient to an orthopedic or other specialist who can provide more intensive help. Acknowledging a deficiency and outsourcing the patient does not make this doctor appear weak or unprofessional. It shows she cares enough about the patient to seek the quality care needed to improve the condition. In many instances, educators should follow the same lead. We should not allow our biases, convictions, or desires to appear in control to hinder us from getting students to the appropriate people to help them. Additionally, educators cannot feel they are so professional and be tricked into thinking they are experts about things they are not. If our bias or lack of knowledge relative to a matter limits our ability to be empathetic and help certain students, we should be professional enough to own up to it. We should not be too proud to outsource or explore external resources that can help our students. Claiming our biases and the extent of their influence in our decisions can go a long way when it comes to our ability to meet our students' needs.

Bias Reflection & Intervention

Belief/Bias	Degree	Consideration	Compromise Initiative
Ex. Students who wear pants below their waist.	1st	1. No belt 2. Parents buy their clothes big to avoid buying so many clothes. 3. Parents may not know their child is not wearing a belt. 4. The kids may only see people who wear pants that way.	1. Get extra belts from neighbors, colleagues, etc. to keep in the classroom. 2. Private conversations with him/her about attire. 3. Celebrate when he/she wears pants appropriately. 4. Constructive phone calls home.

Points of Reflection

As educators, it is essential that we check our bias and prejudice at the door before entering homes, schools, and districts. We also need to realize how much impact personal, societal, and systemic bias has on the academic standards, behavior codes of conduct, and overall policy relative to our schools. Doing so will go a long way in helping us to assess our cultures and create more welcoming environments for children and families to pursue access to the resources they need for achieving greater success. Every student deserves full and equitable access regardless of race, religion, gender, socioeconomic status, etc. They are also deserving of this right despite how others may feel about their home environment, upbringing, or classroom behavior. So, it is indeed critical to ensure that our biases do not interfere with granting students access to school resources that can potentially help them. This is just as important as meeting their academic needs. Further, we should not allow personal, societal, or systemic bias to influence decisions on the depth or frequency of granting students access to these resources.

Being aware of the extent of biases (first, second or third degree) and how they influence our thinking and approaches will allow us to be more cognizant of the impacts of our decision-making relative to school and classroom protocol and policy. Schools and classrooms that are tainted with bias-filled procedures or policy will do more harm than good and will create more power struggles between schools, students, and homes. Engaging in these ideological power struggles, especially in the case of student misbehavior, will not change things for the better. In fact, these power struggles do more to show how little power educators have. We may win the battle by sending a student out of the room, having him reprimanded by administration, or getting him assigned to ISS or OSS. However, we quite often lose the war of relationship building because none of these remedies do much in the way of strengthening the relationship once the student returns to the school or classroom. When a student returns to class displaying behaviors that resemble what he or she did before leaving and is now involving other students in those disruptive behavior tendencies, which typically occurs with disgruntled students, it reveals the futility of the power struggle. Additionally, it implies we should perhaps explore other approaches to meet students' needs. We cannot allow biased and vengeance-seeking type notions of retribution (under the pretense of "law and order") to govern our decision-making when considering strategies for dealing with students or in deciding whether to grant them access to resources. If the overall goal is for student growth, abrasive and vigilante style approaches will not achieve that result.

Chapter 4

Confronting the Impact of White Privilege on Systems and Schooling

White privilege discourse offends some and immediately puts them on the defensive, causing rebuttals of false equivalencies as well as other tactics intended to silence or suppress the dialogue. These tactics serve to reduce the significance of White privilege discourse as well as its impact on financial, legal, health care, and educational systems within our culture. It is my sincerest hope this chapter can be objectively read and interpreted, and a healthy discourse can ensue without resorting to tactics of spin, false equivalencies, as well as other associated defense mechanisms intended to discredit the validity and significance of this concept.

Arguably, conversations about White privilege are too often avoided or approached with aggressive confrontation because of the literal connotation. Candidly speaking, I believe the term 'White privilege' is likely offensive to some White people because it somehow suggests White people are the only group of people who are privileged. It may be best to start by decoding and clarifying the semantics that are potentially hindering the willingness to move beyond the terminology and engage in objective discourse about the relevancy of the topic. To be clear, at some point, everyone has "privileges," which *Webster's Dictionary* defines as "a special right or benefit granted to a person." There are instances where privilege is accompanied with a degree of power and influence. However, it is also important to understand that all privilege is not equal in value or grants the same degree of power, access, or influence. So, it is possible to have privilege without having legitimate power, access, or influence to accompany it. However, American history provides a road map for the significant influence White privilege had and continues to have on the balances of power, influence, and access within the foundational systems of our culture.

The Effects of White Privilege on Established Power Structure Norms

Power, oppression, and influence have been cornerstones in erecting this nation. In the early 1600s, land was taken from Native American Indians. During this same period, African slaves were captured and brought to the United States where they were forced to provide free labor and were subjected to inhumane conditions. The Civil War was fought for the purpose of maintaining power, oppression, and influence over land and people. Once slavery was abolished in the mid-1800s, Jim Crow laws were implemented to prevent Blacks from voting, earning an education or obtaining employment. Additionally, school integration of the early 1950s mostly involved Black students leaving their home schools due to the unequal deficiency of resources and attending White schools. Numerous snapshots of our history provide evidence of the consistent and usually dominant presence of Whiteness and White principles when there are issues, ideas, or platforms involving a distribution of power, access, and influence in our country. While many throughout history have attempted to justify or rationalize this claim, the fact is this has been the case in the past, and it continues to be the case today. However, the issues of inequity and oppression run deeper than the presence of White people's seat at the table of power and influence.

Equity, inclusion, and access conversations should engage stakeholders of various ethnicities, genders, etc. by allowing them a seat at the table so there is increased likelihood for diverse input, in addition to sensible distribution of access, power, and influence. So, the presence of White stakeholders in this type of caucus is necessary. However, out of America's over 200-year history, it has only been within the past several decades that groups other than White people have been legitimately involved and acknowledged as having a legitimate seat at the table. Even with others now having their seat at the table, the usual anticipated outcome is that White opinions, ideologies, and perceptions are the voices that will be amplified and heard more significantly because past experiences have programmed many to accept a reality that White voices will be heard most exclusively. Some choose to push back on this idea by claiming there is a voluntary lack of involvement by groups who now have been given access. While this claim may appear practical, it disregards the realistic perspectives of the people who have been denied involvement in the process for so long.

The Impact of White Privilege on Engagement and Trust

After years of not being acknowledged and being denied the opportunity to actively and equitably participate in the American legal, financial, healthcare, and educational systems, it is barely realistic or practical to expect those who have been alienated to now begin unconditionally trusting and believing in the same system along with believing those who have maintained power and influence within the system. It should be understandable why those who have been alienated would be untrusting and suspicious of the likelihood that those who discounted them for so long are now going to suddenly find value in seeking remedies to make the necessary systemic changes so there is an equitable and inclusive culture for all instead of just the few. Clear examples in history show how dominant the role of White privilege vis-a-vis Whiteness has been in shaping cultural and societal norms and perspectives in America. So, a major first step in achieving the goal of equity, access, and inclusion is a willingness to be realistic about why and how things are the way they are. However, it would be practically impossible to engage in a serious conversation about the influence of White privilege when there are many who either still pretend it does not exist, or they claim it has limited impact on the success or lack of success for other groups.

Despite the claim that there is a lack of involvement by Black, Indigenous, and People of Color (BIPOC) or marginalized groups, the history of White aggression and dominance in our country cannot be ignored, especially as it relates to issues surrounding access, power, and influence. This factor has played an essential role as to why some in minority communities believe White ideologies, opinions, and perceptions will always drown out their voices. So, while more groups now having a seat at the table of equity, access, and inclusion is a great thing, these other factors give validity to why certain minority communities question the power and influence of their voices in such platforms and believe their involvement and feedback are not taken as serious as White voices. Past and present events show that power and influence are crucial elements for gaining the most substantial and irrevocable privilege in this country.

Power, influence, and irrevocable privilege have often been granted to people without regard for equality, equity, or inclusion. You may recall paying to attend certain events and social functions and seeing a celebrity in attendance. In some instances, you may also recall having to stand in a long line to enter the establishment whereas the celebrity was able to gain immediate access to the venue as well as gain immediate access to the establishment's resources. You are paying your hard-earned money to get into the establishment, but because she is famous, the celebrity can attend the same venue, be admitted without hassle (body searches, showing ID., etc.) and gain immediate accessibility to benefits that you, a regular patron, do not have access to.

Imagine that you went to the management of the establishment attempting to express your concerns about the inequitable treatment and access being granted to the celebrity in comparison to the treatment and access granted to common patrons in attendance like you. While the inequity appears obvious, imagine the management responds by saying things such as, "That is the most insane thing that I have heard for you to make that accusation," or, "If you would like the same perks, you should do something to become famous, too." Those responses by management probably would not make you feel you had been heard or that management valued your opinions or concerns. Further, would you have positive feelings about continuing to support that establishment or have any motivation to continue investing your money in the establishment?

Situationally, this scenario is a little different because privileged celebrities come from a variety of racial and ethnic backgrounds. However, conceptually it is important to draw from the above scenario to build a constructive parallel for associating discourse surrounding the power of sustained White privilege. In the above scenario, if you, the claimant, express a concern to management, the respondent, you are more than likely not intending to vilify the celebrity. However, your main point would likely be to bring attention to the noticeable inequities that exist between how attentive the establishment is to the needs of the celebrity, the one with power and influence, versus their attentiveness to the needs of the regular patron. When the inequities are plainly visible and management is accusatory of you and unwilling to acknowledge the disparity in treatment, it would be almost impossible to engage in a healthy conversation about how to improve it or allow you to feel like your issues were taken seriously.

Similarly, the conversations and claims associated with White privilege and inequity are not intended to vilify the White race. They are intended to bring attention to the consequential differences in equitable attention and treatment that are due to a lack of access to resources and amenities that directly and indirectly exist because of the lack of power and influence associated with having a different color skin. The longitudinal presence and significant influence of White privilege within the legal, financial, health care, and educational systems and the historic impact it has on shaping dominant culture norms and perceptions pertaining to these systems can no longer be ignored if there is genuine intention of creating equity and access for all citizens. Because of its historical influence, confronting the existence of White privilege, being attentive to its idiosyncrasies that generate inequity, and revising the norms, protocols, and policies within our systems that have consistently regenerated the power and influence of Whiteness are important steps for society and the educational community. Reflecting upon the celebrity scenario, many of us probably would not bother having the conversation with the management because we have been normalized into believing that power and influence are the benefactors of privilege and access. So, despite how unfair a scenario such as this may appear, the dominant culture has conditioned us to believe and accept that privilege and access should accompany power and influence within American culture.

Sadder yet, scenarios such as these have occurred for years and have continuously engrained in us to unconsciously succumb to power and influence ideologies without questioning principles of access, inclusion, equity or equality. Despite how valuable my words and ideas may be as a common person, I am less likely to gain mainstream access to public platforms to share those ideas (e.g. million Twitter followers, speaking on television shows, etc.). However, if I were rich and famous, having starred in numerous movies, or having done something to put me into the public spotlight, my ideas would have access to immediate public platforms because of the power and influence television and celebrity stardom have in society. Essentially, the historical power and influence of Whiteness and White privilege in our country relative to the legal, financial, health care, and educational systems give similar unwritten privilege and access that is not granted to others of a different skin color. For the sake of building trust between White people and people of marginalized groups, it is essential that

White privilege as well as its influences on dominant culture perspectives and norms be objectively recognized and acknowledged.

Attempting to explain White privilege away or disregard its significance within the systemic power structures continuously perpetuates the fraudulency of the status quo, which contributes nothing toward creating more equitable solutions in leveling the playing field for all groups of people. However, in my experiences, I have witnessed some White people and those who embrace the dominant culture norms attempt to discredit White privilege's impact on equity, access, and equality through a variety of approaches.

Loud and Proud. The goal of this approach is to loudly, boldly, and sarcastically discredit White privilege by making someone feel ashamed for having brought up such a claim. Loudness, belligerence, and sometimes insults are intended to steer conversations about White privilege into a different direction or to even discourage them from being had at all. This approach is characterized by the respondent using aggressive and condescending tones and coercive rhetoric intended to deflect from the impacts of White privilege as well as the associated discourse. For example, someone responding to the suggestion of White privilege claims by stating, "That is the stupidest thing that I have ever heard," is attempting to discredit the claim and belittle the person or group making the claim. The sharp and coercive rhetoric intends to deflect from White privilege discourse by intimidating the claimant enough to immediately shut it down or by provoking a reciprocal coercive response from the claimant, which produces a chaotic shouting and insult competition instead of intelligent discourse about the impacts of White privilege. If either one of these actions is the outcome, the respondent has successfully deflected from the topic and has evaded having to engage in a serious discussion about White privilege.

Whitewash. The goal of this approach is to evade or devalue White privilege discourse by claiming it is a thing of the past and that it has already been dealt with. Because this approach attempts to suggest that the issue of race and skin color has already been addressed, it seeks to diminish its present-day influences over norms, policies, and perspectives. The intention is to downplay the impacts of White privilege, which deflects accountability for having to make changes.

In using this approach, some may attempt to utilize the Civil War, the implementation of Civil Rights laws, and the election of BIPOC citizens into United States congressional, presidential and vice-presidential positions as indicators that our country is beyond the impacts of White privilege and social injustices. While victory in a war, implementation of new laws, and election of BIPOC officials are certainly all steps in a positive direction, those accomplishments by themselves do not ensure that attitudes and perspectives will change for White people who believed for so many years their race or ethnicity is the most powerful and influential, thus, deserving of privilege. Privilege accompanies the thoughts of people who believe this way, and independent acts such as winning the Civil War, implementing Civil rights laws, or electing BIPOC officials is unlikely to change deeply embedded mindsets such as these.

When attempting to create an equitable culture, it becomes especially detrimental if those who think this way are in positions of authority (e.g. CEOs, executive directors, school leaders, etc). While elections and new legislation are essential resources in shifting the privilege paradigm, more actions are necessary to increase systemic accountability for doing so. The Whitewash Approach seeks to delegitimize the current existence and influence of White privilege through implying that enough has been done to shift and reduce its impacts as well as the overall impacts of Whiteness. However, creating more equitable, accessible, and inclusive environments requires more than referencing remote circumstantial events as a superficial basis for proving that BIPOC and marginalized people now fit into this society with the same degree of power and privilege as White people. Regardless of how many wars are fought, laws are passed, or elections are won, no meaningful change will occur unless the attitudes and mindsets of the people, especially those in possession of power, influence, and privilege, change first. Undoubtedly, winning wars for emancipation and passing laws to address equality and access have moved us in a right direction, but the next steps for reducing the impacts of White privilege and improving equity have to be personal, organizational, and systemic accountability.

Both Sides Approach. This is a common approach utilized to deter, undermine, or spin discussions surrounding inequity and privilege. The goal is for the respondent to lessen the claim of White privilege by highlighting the deficiencies on the other side for the purpose of avoiding unwanted accountability. This approach attempts to dismiss talks of inequity, injustice, and White privilege by claiming that inequity, injustice, flaws, as well as privilege is just as prevalent on the other side. This approach also uses false equivalencies to delegitimize the prevalence of White privilege.

For example, some are quick to say how their ancestors came to this country with nothing, but they were able to change their fortunes due to hard work ("lacing up my bootstraps.") This type of claim is usually specific to Black people, and it is utilized to argue that if White people's, and other ethnic groups' ancestors could come here with nothing, work hard, and gain something for themselves, it would be expected that Black and other marginalized groups of people should be able to do the same. Specific to Black people, this is an apparent and insulting false equivalency because White people's ancestors did not come to this country in the bondage that Black people's ancestors did. White people along with most other ethnic groups had the privilege of coming to this country of their own free will and actively pursuing wealth and prosperity from the onset, whereas Black people's ancestors did not. This does not intend to make light of White or other groups' ancestorial struggles, but history shows us that Black people's ancestors had to first struggle for freedom before they could even think about actively pursuing wealth and prosperity. So, this factor alone would have a substantial generational impact on Black people's abilities to acquire wealth, privilege, power, education, and influence that White people and other cultures already had access to. An attempt to make a generalized equivocation between White and Black people's ancestorial experiences to justify the wealth, power, education, and prosperity gaps in this country would be an apparent false equivalency. Also, making such a claim likely perpetuates further interracial distrust because it indirectly suggests that laziness and apathy are the primary reasons for Black and other marginalized group's lack of success.

Instead of seriously engaging in discourse concerning inequity, injustice, or privilege, this approach intends to generate a stalemate, thus, giving the justification for why nothing should have to change. In the respondent's mind, this places the accountability discussion back into the claimant's lap, and it also establishes justification for why the respondent should be excluded from accountability. By doing so, those respondents with the dominant culture perspective are suggesting that the claimant's assertion of inequitable or unjust treatment is not credible because the other side, which is most probable to be the side of the claimant, is just as wrong, guilty, or negligent. Therefore, the claimant should not be attempting to lay blame on the respondent for inequitable or unfair treatment because they display behaviors and tendencies that are just as bad. If this approach is successful, it will create a stalemate scenario which suggests that nothing needs to be investigated or changed.

Awareness and Accountability

The previously mentioned approaches are self-defined through my experiences and interactions with White people, Whiteness, and White privilege. So, they more than likely will not be identified by these specific names in research articles or reports. However, it is important to call these tactics out to increase awareness of why such approaches are utilized and how they influence discourse because they contribute to an ongoing inability to make necessary changes. Dominant culture has no problem with assigning the blame for financial, legal, and educational under achievements of BIPOC and marginalized students and families to apathy, dysfunction, laziness, etc. If we are serious about improving equity, access, and inclusion for ALL and leveling the playing fields in the financial, legal, healthcare, and educational systems, White privilege and its influences need to be called out just as assertively. That means people should stop attempting to suppress or delegitimize the impacts of White privilege within organizations and systems.

There are some White people who honestly may not be aware of the role and magnitude of their privilege in addition to the impact it has on their access to resources or simply their access to being given the benefit of the doubt that other people different from them do not receive. However, some White people assertively utilize various approaches to maintain their privilege because they understand that having privilege also means possessing access to a degree of power and influence. That is why those who think this way see it as beneficial to pretend it does not exist. This is not to suggest that life is a bed of roses for White people because there are certainly poor White people in our country in the same way there are poor

Black, Indigenous, and People of Color. However, the suggestion here is that in consideration of all superficial things being equal, White privilege grants White people, whether poor or affluent, a more likely opportunity for receiving the benefit of the doubt and access to certain tangible as well as ideological resources quicker because of their Whiteness. The only way to shift this paradigm is to openly acknowledge its existence and hold organizations and systems accountable for changing them.

What good is it to post a speed limit and minimum sign if no one monitors or stops drivers to ensure they are held accountable? While speed limit and minimum laws may have good intentions, they are not worth very much if very few people follow them or are held accountable if they violate them. The same could be said for other laws as well, but the point here is that while creating laws and credence may have the best of intentions (e.g. Emancipation Proclamation, Civil Rights laws, etc.), they have minimal organizational or systemic effectiveness if they are not diligently scrutinized and people do not feel they will be held accountable for governing themselves within the parameters of those established ordinances. To give acknowledgement to a group of people and their rights through legal and societal doctrines without also implementing prudent accountability structures designed to actively monitor, check, and balance ethical compliance would be just as ineffective as the speed signs where barely anyone gets stopped (limited accountability). Factors such as these are especially relevant when it comes to schooling in our country.

The Impact of White Privilege on the Power Structures of Schooling

It is essential our educational community is a catalyst for engaging in serious professional discourse and analysis pertaining to White privilege, privilege-based cultures, as well as any other potentially oppressive devices if meaningful change is expected to occur with meeting the needs of ALL students. Specifically, the influence of White privilege and its impact on dominant culture perspectives relative to curriculum, day-to-day pedagogy, and evaluation as well as policy aspects of schooling require educators to truthfully confront them if there are serious intentions of improving achievement. As previously mentioned, the reality is when it comes to discourse surrounding White privilege along with other factors that significantly impact student achievement, socioeconomics, student trauma, socioemotional development to name a few in the education system, it is often difficult to get answers or engage in meaningful dialogue because educational accountability seems to be associated with improving grades, raising test scores, and adding more bells and whistles to the academic curriculum. That means elements outside of those three dimensions are usually neglected, and teachers, schools, and district officials are forced to deal with the other neglected issues on their own.

In the same way that privilege grants celebrities overt and covert rights and access, White privilege also grants most White people numerous special rights and benefits that have given them direct and indirect access to influence over policies, principles, and perceptions existing within the systems of America. An abundance of evidence proves the privilege and power narrative created by White privilege is what shapes and fuels the educational system and the bureaucracy associated with it. That is why the only things that have seemed important in education are grades, test scores, and intricate curriculums. Consequently, the only students who have been considered successful are the ones who make good test scores and decent grades and show diligence in mastering the curriculum standards – the high-test scoring honor roll students who rarely or never cause discipline problems.

Because discourse surrounding the influences of power and privilege within the current educational system have been overlooked, the same ideologies and stigmas are consistently perpetuated. The result is students who fall into the good grades, high test score, and minimal behavior problem categories, dimensions that are revered in the educational system designed for the empowered and privileged, continue experiencing success while the outlier students or the ones who struggle in any or all these same categories continue to fail, underperform, or go unrecognized for their achievements. This is where it becomes necessary to understand that all privilege, especially relative to the education system, is not equal.

A remedial special education student has special rights, benefits, and access that other students do not have, but their power and influence relative to the structures associated with success in many schools is minimal. While these students may have privilege, and a degree of power resulting from their IEPs, the privilege and power they possess is not directly or indirectly influential enough to compel numerous districts and schools to equitably reconsider their criteria of expectations for what a successful student should look like. In simpler terms, newly erected grade schools are more likely to actively recruit and tout the honor roll or gifted and talented students who apply and attend the school than they are to recruit and tout the remedial special education students. A remedial special education student may be considered privileged, but her privilege will not have the same degree of indirect or direct power and influence in schools that an honor roll gifted-and-talented (GT) student has.

Some may challenge this claim and say the remedial special education student possesses just as much power and influence due to her legally binding Individualized Education Program (IEP). While this student's IEP may give her and her parents power and influence, it is not comparable to the power and influence of most honor roll GT students. After all, most schools have protocol in place to publicly celebrate and recognize achievements and accomplishments of honor roll and GT students whereas the same cannot be said for remedial special education program students. A significant number of districts and schools conduct honor roll, top 10%, and a variety of other academic club-related ceremonies to acknowledge the specific accomplishments and achievements of honor roll, GT, and other categories of high performing and well-behaved students. However, in many districts and schools it would be a struggle to find the same volume of recognitions and celebrations for remedial special education students and outlying students who may struggle with grades, performing well on tests, or behavior issues. Our educational system of privilege, power and influence has conditioned us to be quick to find reasons to scrutinize these types of students while being reluctant to find reasons to celebrate and praise them.

Many remedial special education students, low test scoring students, and students with mediocre grades or behavior make gains and achievements throughout an academic quarter, semester, or year, but their accomplishments do not garner the same attention unless they measure up to the criteria of success that has been established by the privilege, power, and influence system. When this is the case within an educational culture, it proves that the power, influence, and privilege of these students are not comparable to that of the honor roll, GT students, and high performing students. Consequently, this creates educational cultures where labeling and stigmatizing students and families become more of the priority than finding opportunities to actively recognize, empower, and celebrate them.

It is up to the educational community to recognize this disparity if it exists. It is up to teachers and educational leaders to understand the impact of privilege, power, and influence dynamics so protocol can be revamped and reestablished to equitably recognize and celebrate the achievements of more categories of students than just those who conform to the criteria of the status quo. Failure to recognize these differences and revise protocol, where applicable, would be to support the way things always have been and to support the same results. One of the most obvious disparities relative to the power and privilege structure is in school discipline systems. Although Black and White students are generally reprimanded for similar infractions, Black students are suspended and expelled at higher rates than White students. This being true, it is logical to conclude that White students are given the benefit of the doubt, tolerance, or pardons for infractions that Black students are not given. The bigger and more consequential question is if the influences and benefits of privilege (White privilege in this case) noticeably impact perceptions, protocol, and policy relative to student discipline in education, how many other systems and educational programs has it also infiltrated? Serious discourse about creating equitable cultures means there is the willingness to identify influences of power and privilege and mitigate its associated benefits so the educational community can level the playing field to sensibly generate solutions for increasing equity and access in all areas of education.

Points of Reflection

For those who are offended because of the title of this chapter or of how frequently White privilege is referenced as one of the problems hindering the educational community from increasing equity, access, and inclusion, seemingly, you are missing the bigger picture and the overall premise for why this chapter was constructed. First, White privilege and its impacts on school culture, school perspectives, and student achievement is ONE of the problems. While it is not the only problem (as others will be identified and discussed throughout this book), the impact of White privilege is a significant problem influencing the educational system that has not been adequately addressed because of the sensitivity that some tend to have when the topic arises.

For years, BIPOC, marginalized students, and families have heard the suggestion that their apathy, dysfunction, and laziness are the primary reasons for their predicaments. Marginalized families and communities have repeatedly heard this rhetoric and have been expected to take ownership of it when it comes to doing something to better their own situations. Similarly, White people and dominant culture should be willing to openly acknowledge the presence of White privilege in our culture and systems and take ownership in mitigating its impacts, especially if it is a catalyst for inequity. As it relates to poverty, incarceration, and underachievement, the dominant culture has a conditioned response of immediately blaming the recipients of these consequences. However, there is rarely the same degree of emphasis placed on scrutinizing the policies and ideologies of organizations and systems and how those practices may contribute to pre-existing as well as existing problems. It is time to create a paradigm shift where personal sensitivities and biases are set aside so we can more actively do the work of acknowledging and seeking resolutions for ALL problems that contribute to hindering student growth and student achievement.

Specifically, our purpose as educators should be to do whatever is necessary to increase the likelihood of student growth and success. The reality is it will be easier to achieve this for some students, and it will be more challenging to achieve for others. However, creating equitable cultures requires taking ownership and accountability for all factors that impact student growth and achievement. It means we need to stop denying the power and influence of White privilege in the education system and its impacts on the various systems in this country. Tactics intended to assign blame, guilt, shame, or apathy will not improve the quest for equity, inclusion, and access, especially in education. Some evade White privilege discourse unknowingly, but there are others who evade it intentionally because they are aware of the power and influence of White privilege as well as how it benefits their specific cause or narrative. However, it is essential to acknowledge and understand the importance of mitigating White privilege and its impacts on organizational and systemic structures so there can be a level playing field for all groups and individuals who desire to be successful. Being nonchalant and acquiescing to the same tactics of reasoning for why things should remain the same will continue producing distrust, disenfranchisement, and inequity.

#equityoverprivilege

Chapter 4 Reflection Questions

What (if any) specific areas of your classroom, school, or district consist of high disparities of adverse outcomes or performances by Black, Indigenous, and People of Color (BIPOC)?

What has the classroom, school, or district concluded is the source of the disparity of adverse outcome(s) associated with BIPOC students?

What plans or programs have been implemented by the classroom, school, or district to remedy the disparities existing for these students?

Setting	Area of Disparity	Plan(s) of Action
Classroom		
School		
District		

Chapter 5

Taking Ownership for Being First Responders

I recall being at a school for a student meeting. After the meeting, another behavior interventionist and I were called to assist with a situation involving a troubled student. The student was not doing what she was told to do because she really did not want to be at school or comply while there. The student was only in elementary school at the time, but she had been to at least four other schools, including a couple outside of the county. The student's home life was not the most stable and there was not a significant level of home support.

Due to physical threats of harm she was making towards herself, the interaction with this student took a turn to the point where emergency medical technicians (EMTs) were called. When the other behavior interventionist and I entered the room where the student was, one of the EMTs was attempting to negotiate with the student to get her to stand up. Having been trained in crisis intervention techniques, we attempted to assist the emergency team member with getting the student up. While we attempted to support the student's arms, the emergency team member was down near the student's legs. The student began kicking wildly and subsequently kicked the emergency team member in the chest. While we could tell the emergency team member was perturbed after being kicked, rather than disengaging or responding with a snide remark or gesture, she resumed her efforts of assisting with transporting the child to a safer space where she could receive the services she needed.

In revisiting the above scenario, the EMT, the first responder, continued providing the best service she knew how to provide for the child despite having just been kicked in the chest.

It would have been much easier (and probably felt better) for the EMT to wipe her hands of the entire situation and begin speaking and thinking negatively about the student or the student's family. However, she continued engaging with the student to provide her with the quality care she needed, a prime example of what first responders must do in many instances. I can only imagine how many times this emergency team member may have encountered a situation where the victim or patient did not want to be transported to the emergency room or receive the care that is required to give all patients. While the situation or circumstance that created the emergency is not something emergency team members have control over nor are responsible for, their job, if done with fidelity, still requires them to provide the patient with the utmost care and service. So, while they may encounter a person who drank himself into a health problem requiring emergency assistance, it is not first responders' jobs to make a judgement call about the patient's character, family, or values. Their job is to do the best they can in getting that patient back to good and stable health in hopes the patient may get another chance to get it right the next time.

As educators, it is imperative we consider ourselves through a similar lens. It is a certainty that at some point the students we serve (our patients) will refuse, rebut, or resist the content and character lessons we attempt to teach. However, we should not be content with disengaging from them just because of this occurrence. Regardless of whether the patient created the problem or not, an EMT's level of engagement with their patients will significantly influence whether that patient lives or dies. Thus, it is imperative we as educators do not lose sight of the value and importance of remaining engaged with the students we serve because the quality of our interaction could be the difference between a student having successful learning experiences versus having unsuccessful ones. Frequently, student refusal, rebuttal, or resistance is their way of crying out that they need help, and educators do a disservice to students when they disengage from these students rather than persevere and do their part in meeting these students' needs.

Resource for Taking Ownership and First Response – Interest Inventories

Educators spend a considerable amount of time conducting initial, interim, formative, and summative assessments with students. In all subjects, reading, writing, math, science social studies, etc., it is essential to get an idea of students' academic knowledge in order to know where instruction should begin. Whether it is state test scores, diagnostic tests, or reading level, there always seems to be some type of data or assessment tool that guides us when it comes to teaching standards to students, but how much time do we spend doing this as it relates to gaining personal knowledge of each student so we can make informed decisions on how to interact and effectively mentor them? Alienating the experiences, personal details, and intricacies of students will subsequently hinder the capacity to boost their achievement because the details associated with their personal lives and experiences influence how they interact and learn. Without learning the details about our students' lives, it will make it more of a challenge to build rapport and relationships with them and meaningfully teach and mentor them at the highest level.

Comparable to academic diagnostic tests and assessments, an interest inventory questionnaire helps educators to acquire knowledge about their students. Gaining access to this data will go a long way in helping administrators, teachers, and other staff members in effectively tailor-making instructional as well as interactional experiences with students that generate the most productive outcome. Through conducting interest inventories and engaging in dialog with students and their families, educators will be more equipped with knowledge about their students that can help with avoiding unnecessary disciplinary challenges or counterproductive school experiences that deter rather than accelerate achievement.

"The Interest Inventory Questionnaire" on the next couple of pages can be used to initiate gathering data on your students. There are also items within the questionnaire that should be used as follow up questions for later (in the month/quarter/year) collaboration with students. This resource is by no means intended to be an exhaustive list, and the format as well as structure may need to be adjusted to accommodate different grade levels. It is important to note that interest inventories such as these should not only be used at the beginning of the year. "Getting to Know You" and "Q and A" activities are frequently used in schools and classrooms as warm and fuzzy beginning of the year activities, but they are soon abandoned after the first week or two of school. Please keep in mind the goal of the interest inventory is to obtain useful data that will help in creating meaningful learning experiences and welcoming school and classroom environments for students. So, using an interest inventory at the beginning of the year without revisiting, updating, as well as analyzing the data throughout the year (as we do with academic data) will not be useful. If the plan is to conduct interest inventories and use the data for instructional and interactive decision making, educators should commit to consistently using and updating the data as it should be an iterative process.

Interest Inventory Questionnaire

Student Name: _____

Initial Questions

- What is the main thing that you would like for someone to know about you or your family?

-When is your birthday and what would you like to do to celebrate your birthday?

-How many siblings do you have?

-What are the names of the people in your house?

-Who do you feel is most dependable in your house and why?

-Who is your role model or your favorite person? Why is he/she your role model or favorite person?

-Who is your favorite person to talk to (phone or in person)?

-Do you have a coach? If so, what's his/her name?

-What is the most exciting place that you have ever been and what did you like most about that place?

-If you could make a wish and go anywhere, where would it be? Why?

-What is your favorite food?

Career and School Interest/Hobbies Questions

-What would you like to do once you finish school and you are an adult?

-Does what you want to do require you to go to college?

-Do you plan to go to college? Why or why not?

-If you plan to go to college, what college would you like to attend? Why?

-What do you think is the most important thing for me to know about you and your family?

-What do you like to do when you go outside?

-What do you like to do when you are inside?

-What is your favorite sport?

-What is your favorite thing to do?

-What is your favorite television show?

-Who is your favorite actor or actress?

-What is your favorite type of music?

-Who is your favorite singer or music group?

-Have you ever been to a music concert?

-What is your favorite mobile phone app?

-What is your favorite video game?

-Do you like to read? Why or why not?

-Do you like to write? Why or why not?

-Do you like math? Why or why not?

-Do you like doing experiments?

-What is your favorite subject? Why do you like this subject the most?

-What is the title of the last thing that you read?

Teacher Follow-Up Questions

-Tell one thing that has changed about you or your family since we last spoke?

-Has the number of people who live in your house changed since we last spoke?

-Has anyone in your house changed jobs since we last spoke?

-Is there a certain part about school that you would like to see improved?

-How do you feel about your grades (good or wish they were better)?

-As your teacher, what can I do to help you improve your grades?

-As your teacher, what can I do to help improve your school experience?

-As your teacher, what can I do to help school to be more exciting, interesting, or engaging for you?

-Have you discovered any new hobbies since the last time we spoke?

-Have you done anything that you are very proud of since the last time we spoke?

-Has anything happened that made you afraid or sad since the last time we spoke?

Educator: "Be sure to let me know if there is anything I can do to help you with your success and thank you for the conversation!"

Points of Reflection

If you are an educator who has grade school-aged biological children or stepchildren, you know there are times they have challenged your requests, altered protocols or expectations to fit their convenience, or outright defied your expectations. However, the logical assumption is your approaches for handling issues such as these was not to give up on your children or to take your hands off them and allow them to go it alone. Even during times of contention, defiance, or misunderstanding most parents have an unconditional love and compassion for their children that will not allow them to intentionally alienate their children, deprive them of essential resources, or subject them to circumstances of inevitable harm. This creates a nurturing culture of love and trust in your home because your children know that despite how angry or disappointed you may become with them, they have assurance you will do what is best for them.

As educators, an abundance of the students we serve either do not experience that type of nurturing experience at home or they experience it from a different lens. Either way, whether our students follow the rules the first time or have to bump their heads against the wall 10 times, it is essential that we take ownership in being their first responders and show that we are fully invested in them and their success. Thus, it should never be considered okay or justified to alienate students (academically or behaviorally), turn our backs on them, or be vengeful towards them. Anyone in the educational community who only shows compassion to the students who get it right or comply the first time while showing stern and coercive rebuke to remedial or repeat offending students lessens our chances of creating the nurturing cultures needed for maximizing achievement. By no means does this suggest that we create cultures where consequences do not exist. However, as it relates to our approaches, we should always ask ourselves are we choosing it to satisfy our desire for vengeance, retribution and to follow standardized protocol, or are we choosing it because it is what is in the best interest of the student? Saying this is certainly a lot easier than doing it at times, but the more our students see and believe we are with them through the good and the bad, many of them will embrace consequences with less contention and will be more likely to give us their best.

Chapter 6

We Cannot Have It Both Ways – Foundations for Creating Equitable Culture

More than likely, anyone who chooses to be in education already accepts the fact they will not receive tangible perks and benefits that equate to the time and effort they give to the profession. Through personal experience, most educators have probably witnessed the hypocrisies related to bureaucratic expectation because the level of expectation placed on educators is usually higher and unparalleled to what the bureaucracy is willing to give in return when it comes to meeting the needs (compensation, resources, etc.) of educators. Within our industry of education, there are indeed countless instances where bureaucratic leaders, laws, and policy expect more from educators and the educational community than they are willing to give. The hypocrisy of this messaging is seemingly obvious because having one level of expectation when it comes to what is expected while procrastinating with meeting the needs and expectations of educators and the educational community is inconsistent, hypocritical, and inequitable.

It was important to start this chapter off with affirming these educational challenges because it probably seems as though the majority of this book has been devoted to convicting educators and holding the educational community responsible for the achievement gaps that exist for many students. As I stated at the beginning of this book, I am an advocate for educators (the administrators, teachers, and support staff) who put it on the line every day in hopes of growing students and making a positive difference in their lives. So, yes, I am very much aware there are challenges beyond the control of the educational community that contribute to the gaps and underperformance relative to student achievement. Additionally, challenges and factors such as these contribute to the fatigue many educators feel because they have a genuine desire to improve student performance, but they feel their hands are tied in many instances because of the limited resources available to achieve such a limitless task. While bureaucratic challenges of hypocrisy and double standard may often contribute to an already daunting task of improving student achievement, we should be mindful not to become the beast we so often criticize.

Many educators believe the bureaucracy places too much emphasis on standardized test scores when it comes to measuring student achievement. While most evaluations consist of multiple performance indicators to assess performance, most educators know that student test performance is the bottom line and the indicator that is most relevant in the eyes of the bureaucracy. A significant number of those in the educational community believe (rightfully so in my opinion) that heavy reliability on a test score is an ineffective and unfair practice for interpreting student progress and achievement. Many believe, for example, that it is unreasonable to expect a fifth-grade student who is working on a second-grade level to meet fifth-grade standardized testing criteria by the end of an academic year. Additionally, heavy reliance on test scores does not paint a full picture of the countless times a teacher may have stayed after school to give a student extra help or the times the teacher may have had to talk the student off of an emotional cliff in order to get him to refocus on and reengage with the learning goal for the day. Seemingly, these as well as other examples suggest that educational bureaucrats do not mind measuring educators using inequitable measuring sticks.

While educators do get an opportunity to evaluate their building administrators through annual surveys, etc., they do not get similar opportunities to frequently evaluate leadership at the state and federal levels. In other words, educators do not have the luxury of using stakeholder performance data to evaluate many bureaucrats. Our only opportunity to do that is in the voting booth, and our vote only serves to impact those who are in balloted positions. I have said all of this to say that politicians and those in power (for the most part) measure educators and the educational community with a different level of scrutiny than they measure themselves. Bureaucratic expectation is high when it comes to educators raising test scores, but those in power seem to have less urgency when it comes to supplying educators with the necessary resources to meet the needs of ALL students. In the eyes of the bureaucracy, teachers are supposed to be satisfied with meager salaries and benefits (because we "should not be in the profession for the money") while educational bureaucrats at the state and federal level receive more perks, and in most cases, more money, although they do not interact with students on a day-to-day basis.

I intentionally wanted to illustrate some of the inequities and double standards we deal with in our profession so it would be easier to create the parallel for us to put ourselves in the shoes of students and their families as we consider how to meet their needs. While people do not enter the educational profession to become millionaires, our salaries should definitely be more than they are, and we should be given tools, resources, and allowances that are commensurate with the value of the job we are expected to do on a daily basis. As an educator, I do not agree with the unreasonableness associated with many of the obstacles and inequities placed upon us. However, it is essential that we, as an educational community, ensure we are not perpetuating the same type of unreasonable and unfair expectations when it comes to our students and their families. We should not complain about unfairness when we understand what it means to be victims of it. In good conscious, we should not perpetuate similar inequities for the things we do control as it relates to students and families. Students and their parents should observe mutual accountability from us. They should see us holding ourselves to the same level of accountability as those things we expect from them.

You Expect Intrinsic Motivation? … Model It…

As educators, we always imply or say directly to students that it is important to be intrinsically motivated and willing to work towards a goal that does not give instant gratification. We want students to understand this concept, but if we complain about the burdens of all we have to do for students outside of the scope of the contract or job description, or we complain about that thing we think is the parent's job to do, we send a message that intrinsic motivation is only lip service. Being an educator provides daily opportunities to positively change and influence lives, and it should be in more than just what we say. It should be in what we model to them. Modeling is an essential part of education, and educators should embrace their opportunities to model the expectation. So, if we model unwillingness in our efforts to meet student needs, we suggest to students and their families that the rigidities of our job description and teaching the standards is most important, and we will fall short in meeting the unique needs of many students. If we expect it from them, students should see us modeling intrinsic motivation in our attitudes and in our deeds. They should see this when we go the extra mile to meet their most essential needs, whether those needs are a part of the lesson plan, duty, assignment, or not.

Inequity, Inequality, and Injustice Cannot Be the Norm

Some pragmatists may argue it is unrealistic to have the same expectation for authority figures because there are certain hierarchies within our society that do not afford us the luxury of holding leaders accountable in the same way they hold us accountable. After all, a police officer who pulls a person over for speeding might be the same police officer seen speeding on the highway when there is no emergency. Additionally, politicians may try to speak to the moral conscious of voters when attempting to solicit their votes yet exploit, embezzle, or practice infidelity in their personal and political lives. These and other types of blatant double standards have historically plagued our society for too long, often causing inequality, inequity, and injustice. Broadly, we are a society of finger pointers, passing the buck, and eluders of accountability, all for the sake of avoiding responsibility. These types of practices have played a significant role in creating and perpetuating many of the social injustices we bear witness to in our society today. When it comes to social justice and equity, we as educators should aim to incorporate practices within our educational settings that promote how justice should look instead of how it actually is because that is the only chance there is of shifting the paradigm.

Staff members are less inclined to comply with administrative protocol and policy if they do not feel their leaders govern themselves by those same expectations. Similarly, students and parents are less likely to be assertive in following school and classroom expectations if they do not see administrators, teachers, and staff members holding each other to the same level of accountability in complying with those same expectations. We should be advocates for school cultures which emphasize equity and justice as well as cultural norms that advance expectations in promoting how society should be instead of promoting the stigmatizing injustices and double standards that have plagued our society for too long. The paradigms of inequity, inequality, and injustice will not shift in our society or educational community if we succumb to embracing them as the normal way of doing business.

Generally speaking, when students consistently violate rules or disrespectfully talk back to a staff member, they receive more immediate and derogatory consequences (ISS, OSS, detention, etc.) for their behaviors than adult staff members who may do the same. Often, educators with the similar reputation of disrespectfully interacting with students, parents, or staff members are given slaps on the wrist or are hailed as "stern" and "no nonsense." It is naïve and unrealistic for us to believe that students and their parents do not notice these distinctions when they occur. How can the educational community expect students and their parents to respect rules, procedures, and protocol if they witness us violating the same thing we proclaim to stand for and are not held accountable? Double standards such as these create distrust and dissension within educational environments, and it lessens the probability for partnership - collective efficacy. Integrity should be the catalyst which prevents us from throwing the book at students and parents under the pretense of enforcing rules if we are cavalier about enforcing our own violations of the same things. If we as an educational community are reluctant or unwilling to hold ourselves as well as other educators, staff members, or leadership to as strict of accountability as we hold many of our students and parents to, it should indicate the need for more equality and equity. Relative to accountability, we should exercise the same metrics, flexibilities, and considerations for our students and families we practice for ourselves and our colleagues.

Mutual and reciprocal environments play a major role in advancing teaching, learning, and ultimately, student achievement. Stakeholders, especially students, should know that everyone, regardless of status or authority, is accountable to the same protocol and expectations. It is difficult to promote the importance of paying attention in class if students see educators on their phones or engaged in off-task conversations during assemblies, class times, etc. Additionally, it is challenging to impress upon students the importance of maintaining self-control when they see educators who blatantly mistreat students or interact with other stakeholders in unproductive or demeaning ways. We as the educational community have little room to get upset and frown upon a student who is displaying sarcasm or condescension if she witnesses educators who are getting away with displaying the same type of behavior. Many students often witness these types of behaviors within their environments outside of school, and yet we say their home environments do not provide the structural protocol and policy frameworks of school settings. So, educational communities should be assertive in taking the initiative to raise the bar and ensure that students see a different standard from us within the educational environment. Additionally, they should see our willingness to consistently evaluate rules, policies, and protocols to ensure compliance is reasonably achievable for ALL stakeholders, not just students and parents, but teachers, staff, and administrators too. After all, who are we to be critical of the impact and influence of students' home lives and their experiences if they witness some of the same dysfunctions within educational settings?

Educational environments that have one set of standards existing for the favorable stakeholders and educators and another set of standards for less favorable stakeholders (quite often nonmainstream and marginalized students and families) will struggle in gaining the positive collaboration necessary for maximizing student growth. Educational settings should take care to not allow the loopholes of the law, rules, and expectations to only benefit those who are in favor or authority while allowing those same rules and expectations to work to the detriment of those who have little favor or authority. If students, parents, and other stakeholders recognize a difference in how rules and expectations are interpreted for one group versus another, it will create a divided and toxic culture that yields limited results in creating meaningful and cooperative interaction that is essential for maximum student achievement.

Zero Tolerance Means Zero Tolerance…for EVERYONE

A student whose parent is a board member should not be treated any differently than the student who comes from a single-family home with multiple siblings or the student who has a track record of troubled behavior. If there is an unwillingness for educational communities to equally police ALL stakeholder behavior relative to zero tolerance policy, it might suggest that zero tolerance is not the appropriate accountability metric for this particular rule or protocol. After all, it cannot be considered fair to enforce a policy or expectation for certain students and families while it is not being diligently enforced with students and families who are considered in 'good standing.' Ultimately, double standards relative to behavior and policy will create a further divide between educational stakeholders.

It goes without saying that zero tolerance is a necessity for certain rules and policies existing within educational settings. There should be no debate or consideration required for students or adults who sell drugs or bring bodily harm to someone on a school campus. However, the vast majority of rules, policies, and protocols existing in educational settings are open to subjective interpretation, and the final say usually falls in the hands of the accuser, who is quite often the one in authority. Educational communities attempting to enforce zero tolerance or any other protocol and policy for students and families should be just as zealous with enforcing the policy and protocol for ALL stakeholders regardless of their status, background, role, etc. Enforcement of policy should mean similar accountabilities for ALL. Engaging in this practice helps to create an organizational culture where stakeholders can be confident in meaningful checks and balances, and it should compel most of its members to take a deeper sense of ownership in self-reflective accountability.

Resource for Evaluating Protocol and Policy – Policy Reflection Tool

It is easy to adopt the practice of enforcing policy, rules, and protocol because it speaks to our human desire to have authority, power, or control over our territory. However, it is just as easy to unconsciously put rules, policy, and protocol in place year over year without evaluating effectiveness. As an educational community, rules, policies, etc. significantly influence too many lives, and ultimately, achievement, for them to be impulsively or arbitrarily put into place just to satisfy a checklist or because "they have always been the rule." It is important to engage in meaningful collaboration and use relevant data when evaluating whether enforcement is reasonable and sustainable. Creating more partnership-oriented educational settings will require the educational community to responsibly scrutinize our ability to model and adhere to the same guidelines and principles we expect because we should not expect diligent outcomes if we engage in less than diligent practices.

"The Policy Reflection Tool" can assist educational settings in evaluating rules, protocol, and expectations to ensure reasonable and equitable practices are taking place. The core competencies required to effectively use this tool are collaboration, reflection, feedback, and modification (where applicable). The tool will be most effective if stakeholders work in diverse committees, and while the reflection tool can be used to evaluate any existing rules, policies, and procedures, it should target the most frequently violated ones first. While the format of the committee interaction may be structured differently to meet the unique needs of each educational setting, it should be all inclusive – meaning that administrators, parents, students, teachers, and all other staff members should be afforded the opportunity to participate in this reflective process.

Once the committee uses data to identify the most frequently violated rules, policy, etc., they will identify it, in its entirety, in the appropriate space in the table. Next, they should discuss and address the items within the table as a basis for determining how influential the rule or policy is relative to school governance. For example, zero tolerance policies and rules will usually have stiffer consequences than those rules that are not. So, it will be especially important to evaluate those criteria with a heightened level of scrutiny to ensure the absence of subjectivity or favoritism. Lastly, the committee should determine whether modifications are needed for the specific policy and provide a description of the proposed modification.

When using this tool, it is important to get perspectives from a diverse sample of stakeholders. Factional solidarity – the principle where certain groups or factions feel the need to stick together so as not to weaken the authority or reputation of the group - has overtaken some educational communities. There should be collective rather than factional solidarity in educational settings. So, this tool will be ineffective if perspectives are only presented and considered from one faction's perspective. Involving mainstream along with nonmainstream students and parents as well as a variety of staff members in this process is essential in order for it to be effective. Truthfully, it will take sweat equity to be intentional with organizing diverse committees, but it will make the process and outcome more meaningful because it will create opportunities for stakeholders to work in an objective and productive partnership for the betterment of school culture.

Policy Reflection Tool

Review Date: _____

Rule, Policy, Protocol (List Completely): _____

_____

Zero Tolerance (Yes/No)	Student/Family Consequences (If Violated)	Staff Consequences (If Violated)	Modifications Required (Yes/No)

Suggested Modifications (N/A if no modifications are required): _____

_____

_____

_____

Reviewed By: _____

_____

Points of Reflection

I began this chapter by using relatable professional experiences and scenarios as a basis for connecting with many in the educational community who can relate to the strict and high volume of pressures of bureaucratic expectation. More specifically, the expectations from bureaucrats are usually more extensive than the output of resources they are willing to promise or provide when it comes to meeting the needs of educators as well as the needs of the educational community. Whether it be in education or in society, certain hypocrisies are seemingly obvious, but unfortunately, many of them continue to exist. Ultimately, cultures where sides expect more than they are willing to give create accusatory and blame-filled environments with minimal accountability and the inability to meaningfully listen to the other side. As educators, we probably have experienced being in a space where we felt deprived or slighted of the tools and resources we needed (i.e. more instructional time and instructional or human resources), and how we felt when the tool or resource we needed was sparse or nonexistent. When we reflect upon how we felt in those types of situations, it should motivate us to establish educational settings where NO child or family in our classrooms, schools, or districts experience that feeling.

If we want to ensure that students and their families feel a sense of value, engagement, and ownership in our educational settings, it is important they see an equal and equitable playing field for ALL stakeholders. It is unprofessional and unethical to heighten scrutiny and judgement when students and parents do not follow expectations and protocol while playing it down or being lenient on colleagues as well as on ourselves when it comes to following the same expectations. WE CANNOT HAVE IT BOTH WAYS! If specific policy, protocol, or expectation is important enough for us to adopt in holding students and families accountable, it is also essential enough to hold EVERYONE accountable for modeling, including ourselves as educators. While double standard type behavior may not occur in all educational settings, it occurs frequently enough to create division between stakeholders within educational communities. Ultimately, practices which perpetuate divisive cultures will distract stakeholders from achieving the productive organizational vision, which, in our case, should be to maximize student growth and achievement.

We should not stand on the excuse of our title or status as a means of pardoning us from being accountable to the same expectations as students, parents, and more vulnerable stakeholders. If we hold students accountable to a diligent standard of turning assignments in on time, we should be diligent and on time turning in our lesson plans. If we scrutinize parents for the way we witness them talking to students, we should also be critical of ourselves if we decide to utter an unproductive word or insinuation about an unfavorable or challenging student or parent. If our intention is to improve students and our cultures, we should be the premier models for the practices and behaviors we expect, and it is necessary to actively involve students and parents in the process rather than just taking them along for the ride.

#equityandequalityoverhypocrisy

#teambuildsesteem

Chapter 7

Is Being an Educator the Right Profession for You or Is It Just the Right Thing to Do?

Thanks for taking the time as well as some of the constructive criticisms that came along with the journey of reading this book! I am hopeful this text provided fellow educators and constituents of the educational community with practical ideas and strategies so we can be inspired to take meaningful steps in advancing the development and achievement for ALL students, especially those who need us the most. A significant amount of the book probably seemed like a broken record of repetition as it relates to certain themes and principles. However, the repetition of these themes and principles was intentional because our pedagogy should be grounded in the simple perspective of meeting students' needs first. Policy, protocol, bureaucracy, and standards have dominated governance over the way we do things in education for too long. The fact of the matter is if we put students' holistic needs (academic, socioemotional, Maslow's Hierarchy, etc.) first, the goals of higher student achievement and performance outcomes will take care of themselves. The curricular instruction part should become easier to achieve once their needs are met or addressed. However, our preoccupation with policy, protocol, and bureaucratic expectations relative to achieving standards has somehow distracted us from the common denominator that matters most in our profession, our students – **ALL OF THEM, NOT JUST A FEW. ALL** students' successes matter, not just the students who come from actively involved two parent homes. **ALL** students' successes matter, not just the students who are easy to get to know, well-mannered, and follow directions the first time they are given. **ALL** students' successes matter, not just the students whose parents think and believe the same way we do.

As was stated in the introduction, the essential remedies for improving student achievement and outcomes are simple if we place our focus and priority in the right place, on the right approaches, along with using the appropriate instruments for measuring effectiveness. Therefore, if we stand firm in our purpose for being in this profession, it should make pedagogical, policy, and protocol decisions easier to consider and implement. It is time to refocus our efforts on students, their families (major influencers of our students), and become more serious about ensuring that equitable solutions and resources are in place that allow underprivileged, marginalized, and nonmainstream students to experience just as much success in the learning environment as privileged, upper class, well-connected, and mainstream students do.

If we as educators, the adult professionals who have been trained to do this job, feel a sense of disdain and question the perception of our worth when our needs for assistance and resources go unmet, how do we expect students and families to feel when what they see, hear, and feel give them the perception that we are only there to help them pass tests? Sadly, too many students and parents think we are only there to hold them accountable for following rigid protocol and expose them to the grade level standards so they can pass a test. Understandably, teaching the standards and testing proficiency are important aspects of student growth and our annual evaluations, but meeting the holistic needs of students will sometimes require us to look beyond that agenda. Therefore, regardless of your title or status, if there is any student in your educational community who does not feel like you are there to meet their specific needs as individuals first, it should compel you to ask yourself about the message being sent to those students as well as those families. In consideration of the diversity of student backgrounds, all students should feel educators are there to meet their essential individual needs. If they do not feel this way, it will be significantly more challenging to effectively meet their needs as learners and to subsequently heighten their achievement.

Society Complains Now or Society Complains Later

In my experience as an educator, it has become somewhat of a certainty there are two broader complaints existing within our profession as well as society with respect to education. First, there are those who complain about the state of many of today's students. Generally, they complain that today's students and families lack priority, focus, and concern. Their complaint is that many of today's students do not have realistic goals they are willing to sacrifice for and work toward achieving. They feel that many of today's students are unwilling to be attentive or concerned about anything unassociated with video games, social media, or sports. Second, there are those who complain about students who wind up becoming a part of the system. They complain that these students' and families' failures resulted in the spending of unnecessary tax dollars to keep these adults (who were once students) and families up in the penal or welfare system. Either way, there is a baked-in discourse of complaining that exists within society, and it is suggestive of deficient student progress and a lack of educational achievement within our schools.

In truth, we have permitted these societal complaints to trickle into and, in some instances, hijack the discourse within education. While I am not suggesting we pretend as if problems do not exist, educators cannot afford to become a part of the complainers because it is important we spend our time being a part of the solution. Thus, it wastes time for us to feed into the complaining rhetoric around today's students, parents, and test scores because it is imperative we allocate that time towards actively exploring strategies and solutions to shift paradigms. Yes, the work is strenuous, and quite often, we will have to fight to put our biases to the side for the benefit of being more objective. There is always an opportunity to complain, but only cooperation, consideration, and compassion will move us in the direction of finding the right solutions.

Asking and Answering the Important Questions

Some may read this and think I have lost my mind. I can imagine some educators are responding, "It is absurd and unrealistic to hold educators and teachers to the standard of accountability you describe in going this far for students." I whole-heartedly agree! These are bold expectations to ask of educators! While many will have the best of intentions at the beginning of their professional journey as educators, some will unfortunately burnout and tire out along the way. However, the essential question is if we are not willing to bare the load and assume responsibility for going all out for students, especially those who need it the most, who will? The fact is we cannot do and say the same things and expect different results to occur. Changing the state of education requires that dialogue, thinking, and practices evolve, grow, and change so paradigms can evolve, grow, and change. So, if not now, **when**, and if not me, us, and you, then **who**?

Similar to the training for lawyers, doctors, engineers, etc., this is what we, as educators, trained for, earned degrees, and became qualified to do. So, if not us, who will stop the cycles of social promotion - where students move on to the next grade, next teacher, or next school without being socially or academically equipped? If not us, who will stop the cycles of generational dropouts within families? If not us, who will stop those students who are capable of being in regular education settings, but they are placed in special education classrooms due to being misunderstood or misrepresented? The list of questions could go on, but in my humble opinion, the collective answer is it should start with each of us – here and now!

We have heard time and time before that education is a thankless profession. Yes, this profession is HARD!!! From the materialistic, monetary, and even intrinsic perspectives, we consistently are expected to give more than we get because the bureaucracy contends that our reward should be in helping students develop, grow, and achieve. Ideally, we should always be in the mindset of servitude and doing more for students and families, and we cannot allow the confines of our biases or standards-based programs, in addition to other red-tape protocol deter us from actively pursuing the resources to help meet students' needs. Whether students acknowledge it or not, they are relying on us because, in many instances, no one else will go the extra mile for them. Sometimes, spending those few extra minutes with the counselor, mentor, or another person of influence (although it may be outside of the box of norms) may be the difference between a student having the drive and perseverance to finish the school day productively versus spending the remainder of the day or year suspended or expelled. Sometimes, allowing a student in need to grab a snack or a quick bite to eat when he may have arrived too late for the scheduled breakfast time could be the difference between him acting out in class versus actively participating in class.

The focus on standards, protocol, and, in some cases, our bias, has occasionally clouded our judgement and stifled our thinking and ability to be creative in exploring out-of-the-box strategies for meeting needs. That is why it is essential to consistently reflect and evaluate on how these and other factors may potentially influence our instructional practices and approaches. The frequent bouts with shortages of resources already put us at a disadvantage with meeting many of our students' needs, and we can ill afford for anything else to put us at even more of a disadvantage. As educators, if we are unwilling to reflect and acknowledge what we need to change within ourselves, our pedagogy, the institution of education, and how those influences potentially impact the students and families being served, we should respectfully evaluate the passion and desire we have for improving education and for making it meaningful for more than just mainstream students or those who think and believe as we do. Ultimately, there are two types of educators – those who choose the occupation because passion compels them to know it is the right thing for them, or those who choose the occupation because it just seems like the right thing for them to do. If you are truly passionate about this work, one child or group of children left behind is too many. It is each of our tasks to honestly determine which category we fall into and be compelled to act accordingly because if we are in this profession for the right reason, we owe it to ALL students to <u>put each and every one of them first!</u>

Acknowledgements

I am forever thankful to my mother, Alvenes R. Barksdale, who is resting peacefully in heaven, and my father, James Barksdale, who continues to press on and be a living example. My mother was a retired teacher and counselor after a 40-year career. I attribute her passion for students and desire to see each of them be their best to be the inspiration for my passion in doing the same. She was a model educator with a heart of gold! My father has always been a practical do-it-yourself man. He taught me that having knowledge of what is in a book is one thing, but the ability to effectively apply that knowledge in meaningfully solving problems is something else. His practical thinking motivates me to inspire educators and students to do the same, to take the knowledge of research and book-based theory and sensibly apply it to change lives and outcomes.

I stand in awe of this young man daily. My son, Alon Barksdale, and all children like him have been my source of inspiration and motivation for writing this book, doing the research, as well as doing the job that I do every day in working to build more effective and nurturing school cultures for all students. While Alon experienced the challenges of being misunderstood, underserved, and mislabeled due to biases of some teachers and administrators during certain times of his P-12 schooling, he persevered. Through his maturity, he developed an understanding of the importance of valuing his identity, which helped him be more successful. So, to those students who resemble Alon, I challenge you to not let anything or anyone hinder you from achieving the success that you know you are capable of.

While the work it took to accomplish this was Alon's alone, throughout his career in public schooling, he has been fortunate to have two parents who were actively involved in his educational process. Numerous times, it was our presence as parents that played a role in shifting some inequities that were attempted to be levied against him. Unfortunately, there are a significant number of students who do not have this support due to a lack of access to one or both of their parents or because the standards-based and metrics driven cultures that exist within many educational settings have deterred them from being present and involved in their child's classroom or school, which lessens the likelihood of high achievement. To parents, I encourage you to hang in there and stay actively and constructively involved in your child's success in schooling. Mountains will not move and paradigms will not shift without your relentless and consistent involvement in your child's education.

To educators who take it to the limit every day, please be assured that you are not the problem or the villains. With the bureaucratic expectations and the constant push to meet the quantitative number associated with the test score, I can empathize with you about the many challenges of teaching. Additionally, I know that it is challenging to teach children you often do not understand or have difficulty relating to. However, please do not allow bias and misperception to prevail. The outcome of an incarcerated student or an inspired and empowered student is primarily contingent upon what happens at home and, just as importantly, what happens in schools and classrooms. While "Thank You!" is not said often enough, your time, energy, and genuine efforts are very much appreciated. Please be encouraged and inspired to objectively meet students' needs where they are so that you can take them to the heights you know they are capable of aspiring to.

References

Introduction

Baker, L. (2006). Metacognition. Retrieved from http://www.education.com/reference/article/metacognition/.

Deans for Impact (2015). The Science of Learning. Austin, TX: Deans for Impact.

DiTomaso, N., Post, C., & Parks-Yancy, R. (2007). Workforce diversity and inequality: Power, status, and numbers. Annual Review of Sociology, 33, 473–501. Retrieved from:http://www.uni-kassel.de/wz1/mahe/course/module5_4/02_ditomaso07.pdf

Eccles, J. (2006). Expectancy value motivational theory. Retrieved from http://www.education.com/reference/article/expectancy-value-motivational-theory/.

Gallimore, R., & Goldenberg, C. (2001). Analyzing cultural models and settings to connect minority achievement and school improvement research. Educational Psychologist, 36(1), 45–56.

Ghaye, T. (2010). In what ways can reflective practices enhance human flourishing? Reflective Practice: International and Multidisciplinary Perspectives, 11(1), 1–7. doi: 10.1080/14623940903525132

Golden, D. (2006, November 13). Colleges, accreditors seek better ways to measure learning. The Wall Street Journal, pp. B1, B2.

Heitzeg, N. (2009). Education or Incarceration: Zero Tolerance Policies and the School to Prison Pipeline. Forum on Public Policy

Holme, J. (2002). Buying homes, buying schools: School choice and the social construction of school quality. Harvard Education Review, 72(2), 177–205.

Karges-Bone, L. (2016). Rich Brain, Poor Brain: Bridging Social and Synaptic Gaps in Schools. Dayton, OH: Lorenz Educational Press

Marsh, J. A., & Farrell, C. C. (2015). How leaders can support teachers with data-driven decision making: A framework for understanding capacity building. Educational Management Administration Leadership, 43(2), 269–289. doi:

10.1177/1741143214537229

Milanowski, A. T., Kimball, S. M., & Odden, A. (2005). Teacher accountability measures and links to learning. In L. Stiefel, A. E. Schwartz, R. Rubenstein, & J. Zabel (Eds.), Measuring school performance and efficiency: Implications for practice and research (2005 American Education Finance Association yearbook) (pp. 137–162). New York: Taylor & Francis.

Rodgers, C. (2002). Defining reflection: Another look at John Dewey and reflective thinking. Teachers College Record, 104(4), 842–866.

Rodgers, C. (2002). Reflecting-on-the-future: A chronological consideration of reflective practice. Reflective Practice: International and Multidisciplinary Perspectives, 9(2), 177–184. doi: 10.1080/14623940802005525

Rueda, R. (2011). The 3 dimensions of improving student performance. New York, NY: Teachers College Press.

Taylor, R. W. (2010). The role of teacher education programs in creating culturally competent teachers: A moral imperative for ensuring the academic success of diverse student populations. Multicultural Education, 17(3), 24-28. Retrieved from http://libproxy.usc.edu/login?url=http://search.proquest.com.libproxy1.usc.edu/docview/815958395?accountid=14749

1. **Understanding and Applying the Pedagogy of Stakeholder Engagement**

Alexander, P. A., Schallert, D. L., & Reynolds, R. E. (2009). What is learning anyway? A topographical perspective considered. Educational Psychologist, 44(3), 176–192. American Psychological Association, Coalition for Psychology in Schools and Education. (2015). Top 20 principles from psychology for preK–12 teaching and learning. Retrieved from http://www.apa.org/ed/schools/cpse/top-twenty-principles.pdf

Bracket, Marc (2019). Permission to Feel Unlocking the Power of Emotions to Help Our Kids, Ourselves, and Our Society Thrive. New York, NY: Caledon Books

Cates, G. L., Skinner, C. H., Watson, S. T., Meadows, T. J., Weaver, A., & Jac, B. (2003). Instructional effectiveness and instructional efficiency as considerations for data-based decision making: An evaluation of interspersing procedures. School Psychology Review,

32(4), 601-616. Retrieved from http://libproxy.usc.edu/login?url=http://search.proquest.com.libproxy2.usc.edu/docview/61906069?accountid=14749

Dembo, M., & Eaton, M. J. (2000). Self-regulation of academic learning in middle-level schools. The Elementary School Journal, 100(5), 473–490.

Gallimore, R., & Goldenberg, C. (2001). Analyzing cultural models and settings to connect minority achievement and school improvement research. Educational Psychologist, 36(1), 45–56.

2. Messages Matter

Anderman, E. M., Anderman, L. H., Yough, M. S., & Gimbert, B. G. (2010). Value-added models of assessment: Implications for motivation and accountability. *Educational Psychologist, 45*(2), 123-137. Retrieved from http://libproxy.usc.edu/login?url=https://search-proquest-com.libproxy2.usc.edu/docview/742872119?accountid=14749

Bandura, A. (2000). Exercise of human agency through collective efficacy. Current Directions in Psychological Science, 9(3), 75–78.

Corts, K. S. (2007). Teams versus individual accountability: Solving multitask problems Through job design. The RAND Journal of Economics, 38(2), 467–479.

Deans for Impact (2015). The Science of Learning. Austin, TX: Deans for Impact.

Farrell, A. F., & Collier, M. A. (2010). School personnel's perceptions of family-school communication: A qualitative study. *Improving Schools, 13*(1), 4-20. Retrieved from http://libproxy.usc.edu/login?url=https://search-proquest-com.libproxy2.usc.edu/docview/742872926?accountid=14749

Graham-Clay, S. (2005). Communicating with parents: Strategies for teachers. *School Community Journal, 16*(1), 117-129. Retrieved from http://libproxy.usc.edu/login?url=https://search-proquest-com.libproxy2.usc.edu/docview/61933037?accountid=14749

Griffin, B. W. (2002). Academic Disidentification, Race, and High School Dropouts. The High School Journal, 85(4), 71–81. Retrieved from http://www.jstor.org/stable/40364355

King, S. (1993). The Limited Presence of African American Teachers. Review of Educational Research, 63(2), 115-149. Retrieved from http://www.jstor.org.libproxy1.usc.edu/stable/1170470

Kirkpatrick, J. D., & Kirkpatrick, W. K. (2016). Kirkpatrick's four levels of training evaluation. Alexandria, VA: ATD Press.

Marsh, J. A., & Farrell, C. C. (2015). How leaders can support teachers with data-driven decision making: A framework for understanding capacity building. Educational Management Administration Leadership, 43(2), 269–289. doi:

Pajares, F. (2006). Self-efficacy theory. Retrieved from http://www.education.com/reference/article/self-efficacy-theory/.

Wilmore, C. (2009). Explaining the gap: Teacher efficacy and the conceptualization of Minority student achievement Wyrick, A. J., & Rudasill, K. M. (2009). Parent involvement as a predictor of teacher-child relationship quality in third grade. Early Education and Development, 20(5), 845-864. Retrieved from http://libproxy.usc.edu/login?url=http://search.proquest.com.libproxy1.usc.edu/docview/61838946?accountid=14749

Young, M., & Anderman, E. (2006). Goal orientation theory. Retrieved from http://www.education.com/reference/article/goal-orientation-theory/.

3. Confronting Bias

Bateman, M., & Kennedy, E. (1997). Male African Americans, single parent homes, and educational plans: Implications for educators and policymakers. Journal of Education for Students Placed at Risk, 2(3), 229-250. Retrieved from http://libproxy.usc.edu/login?url=http://search.proquest.com.libproxy1.usc.edu/docview/62526979?accountid=14749

Belcher, N. M. Disproportionate suspension of African American students in public schools: A

Delphi study Available from ERIC. (1651840335; ED550266). Retrieved from http://libproxy.usc.edu/login?url=http://search.proquest.com.libproxy1.usc.edu/docview/1651840335?accountid=14749

Behnken, M. P. (2014). Linking ADHD to incarceration among African Americans. The ADHD Report, 22(7), 9-16. doi: http://dx.doi.org.libproxy1.usc.edu/101521adhd20142279

Bensimon, E. (Autumn, 2005). Closing the achievement gap in higher education: An organizational learning perspective, *New Directions for Higher Education*, 131 (special issue), 99–111.

DeFina, R., & Hannon, L. (2013). The impact of mass incarceration on poverty. Crime & Delinquency, 59(4), 562-586. Retrieved from http://libproxy.usc.edu/login?url=http://search.proquest.com.libproxy1.usc.edu/docview/1509085546?accountid=14749

Dowd, A. C., & Bensimon, E. M. (2014). Engaging the "race question": Accountability and equity in US higher education. New York: Teachers College Press.

Farrell, A. F., & Collier, M. A. (2010). School personnel's perceptions of family-school communication: A qualitative study. *Improving Schools, 13*(1), 4-20. Retrieved from http://libproxy.usc.edu/login?url=https://search-proquest-com.libproxy2.usc.edu/docview/742872926?accountid=14749

Ferry, N. M., & Ross-Gordon, J. M. (1998). An inquiry into Schon's epistemology of practice: Exploring links between experience and reflective practice. Adult Education Quarterly, 48(2), 98–112. doi: 10.1177/074171369804800205

Gorski P. (2008). Peddling poverty for profit: Elements of oppression in Ruby Payne's framework. Equity & Excellence in Education, 41(1), 130–148.

Green, P. (2004). The Paradox of the Promised Unfulfilled: Brown v. Board of Education and the Continued Pursuit of Excellence in Education. The Journal of Negro Education, 73(3), 268-284. doi:10.2307/4129611

Griffin, B. W. (2002). Academic Disidentification, Race, and High School Dropouts. The High School Journal, 85(4), 71–81. Retrieved from http://www.jstor.org/stable/40364355

Holcombe-Mcoy, C. (2007). Transitioning to High School: Issues and Challenges for African American Students. Professional School Counselor, 10(3), 253-260.

King, S. (1993). The Limited Presence of African American Teachers. Review of Educational Research, 63(2), 115-149. Retrieved from http://www.jstor.org.libproxy1.usc.edu/stable/1170470

Krathwohl, D. R. (2002). A revision of Bloom's Taxonomy: An overview. Theory Into Practice, 41(4), 212–218.

Maxwell, J. A. (2013). Qualitative research design: An interactive approach (3rd ed.). Thousand Oaks, CA: SAGE Publications McPherson, E. (2011). Moving from separate, to equal, to equitable schooling: Revisiting School desegregation policies. Urban Education, 46(3), 465-483. Retrieved from http://libproxy.usc.edu/login?url=http://search.proquest.com.libproxy1.usc.edu/docview/864941701?accountid=14749

Noguera, P. A. (2008). The Trouble with Black Boys…And Other Reflections on Race, Equity, and the Future of Public Education. San Francisco, CA: Jossey-Bass

Rome, B. S., & Dubnick, M. J. (1987). Accountability in the public sector: Lessons from the Challenger tragedy. Public Administration Review, 227-238.

US Department of Education. (2015). Performance Improvement. Retrieved September 12, 2010 from www.goals.performance.gov/agency/ed

Wallis, J., & Gregory, R. (2009). Leadership, accountability and public value: Resolving a problem in "new governance"? International Journal of Public Administration, 32(3–4), 250–273.

4. Confronting White Privilege and its Influence on Dominant Culture Perspectives

Barksdale, T. (2019). Equitable Schooling for African American Students. Beau Bassin, Mauritius: Lambert Academic Publishing

Bateman, M., & Kennedy, E. (1997). Male African Americans, single parent homes, and educational plans: Implications for educators and policymakers. Journal of Education for Students Placed at Risk, 2(3), 229-250. Retrieved from http://libproxy.usc.edu/login?url=http://search.proquest.com.libproxy1.usc.edu/docview/62526979?accountid=14749

Belcher, N. M. Disproportionate suspension of African American students in public schools: A Delphi study available from ERIC. (1651840335; ED550266). Retrieved from http://libproxy.usc.edu/login?url=http://search.proquest.com.libproxy1.usc.edu/docview/1651840335?accountid=14749

https://en.wikipedia.org/wiki/Black_Lives_Matter#:~:text=Black%20Lives%20Matter%20(BLM)%20is,motivated%20violence%20against%20black%20people

Graham-Clay, S. (2005). Communicating with parents: Strategies for teachers. *School Community Journal, 16*(1), 117-129. Retrieved from http://libproxy.usc.edu/login?url=https://search-proquest-com.libproxy2.usc.edu/docview/61933037?accountid=14749

Griffin, B. W. (2002). Academic Disidentification, Race, and High School Dropouts. The High School Journal, 85(4), 71–81. Retrieved from http://www.jstor.org/stable/40364355

Lang, C. (2020). President Trump Has Attacked Critical Race Theory. Here's What to Know About the Intellectual Movement. Retrieved from https://time.com/5891138/critical-race-theory-explained/

https://www.edweek.org/teaching-learning/teachers-can-take-on-anti-racist-teaching-but-notalone/2020/09?s_kwcid=AL!6416!3!486544088589!b!!g!!&utm_source=goog&utm_medium=cpc&utm_campaign=ew+dynamic+recent%20&ccid=dynamic+ads+recent+articles&ccag=recent+articles+dynamic&cckw=&cccv=dynamic+ad&gclid=EAIaIQobChMI7cCzyvy-7gIViuKzCh1DhwndEAAYASAAEgL8NPD_BwE

https://www.history.com/topics/early-20th-century-us/jim-crow-laws

https://www.history.com/topics/colonial-america/pilgrims

Noguera, P. A. (2008). The Trouble with Black Boys…And Other Reflections on Race, Equity, and the Future of Public Education. San Francisco, CA: Jossey-Bass

Peters, S. (2006). Do You Know Enough About Me to Teach Me: A Student's Perspective: The Peters Group Foundation.

5. Taking Ownership for Being First Responders

Anderman, E. M., Anderman, L. H., Yough, M. S., & Gimbert, B. G. (2010). Value-added models of assessment: Implications for motivation and accountability. *Educational Psychologist, 45*(2), 123-137. Retrieved from http://libproxy.usc.edu/login?url=https://search-proquest-com.libproxy2.usc.edu/docview/742872119?accountid=14749

Bandura, A. (2000). Exercise of human agency through collective efficacy. Current Directions in Psychological Science, 9(3), 75–78.

Bogler, R., & Somech, A. (2004). Influence of teacher empowerment on teachers' organizational commitment, professional commitment and organizational citizenship behavior in schools. Teaching & Teacher Education: An International Journal of Research and Studies, 20(3), 277-289. Retrieved from http://libproxy.usc.edu/login?url=http://search.proquest.com.libproxy2.usc.edu/docview/62073919?accountid=14749

Graham-Clay, S. (2005). Communicating with parents: Strategies for teachers. *School Community Journal, 16*(1), 117-129. Retrieved from http://libproxy.usc.edu/login?url=https://search-proquest-com.libproxy2.usc.edu/docview/61933037?accountid=14749

Peters, S. (2006). Do You Know Enough About Me to Teach Me: A Student's Perspective: The Peters Group Foundation.

Shraw, G., & Lehman, S. (2009). Interest. Retrieved from http://www.education.com/reference/article/interest/.

Scott, S., & Palinscar, A. (2006). Sociocultural theory. Retrieved from http://www.education.com/reference/article/sociocultural-theory/.Wilson, J. P. (2008).

Waters, J. T., Marzano, R. J., & McNulty, B. (2003). Balanced leadership: What 30 years of research tells us about the effect on leadership on student achievement. Aurora, CO: Mid-continent Research for Education and Learning.

6. We Cannot Have It Both Ways - Foundations for Creating Equitable Culture

Anderman, E. M., Anderman, L. H., Yough, M. S., & Gimbert, B. G. (2010). Value-added models of assessment: Implications for motivation and accountability. *Educational Psychologist, 45*(2), 123-137. Retrieved from http://libproxy.usc.edu/login?url=https://search-proquest-com.libproxy2.usc.edu/docview/742872119?accountid=14749

Bandura, A. (2000). Exercise of human agency through collective efficacy. Current Directions in Psychological Science, 9(3), 75–78.

Corts, K. S. (2007). Teams versus individual accountability: Solving multitask problems Through job design. The RAND Journal of Economics, 38(2), 467–479.

Dowd, A. C., & Bensimon, E. M. (2014). Engaging the "race question": Accountability and equity in US higher education. New York: Teachers College Press.

Ferry, N. M., & Ross-Gordon, J. M. (1998). An inquiry into Schon's epistemology of practice: Exploring links between experience and reflective practice. Adult Education Quarterly, 48(2), 98–112. doi: 10.1177/074171369804800205

Gallimore, R., & Goldenberg, C. (2001). Analyzing cultural models and settings to connect minority achievement and school improvement research. Educational Psychologist, 36(1), 45–56.

Ghaye, T. (2010). In what ways can reflective practices enhance human flourishing? Reflective Practice: International and Multidisciplinary Perspectives, 11(1), 1–7. doi: 10.1080/14623940903525132

Golden, D. (2006, November 13). Colleges, accreditors seek better ways to measure learning. The Wall Street Journal, pp. B1, B2.

Griffin, B. W. (2002). Academic Disidentification, Race, and High School Dropouts. The High School Journal, 85(4), 71–81. Retrieved from http://www.jstor.org/stable/40364355

Morse, J. F. (2006). Education as a civil right: The ongoing struggle in New York. Educational Studies: Journal of the American Educational Studies Association, 40(1), 39-59.

Retrieved from http://libproxy.usc.edu/login?url=http://search.proquest.com.libproxy2.usc.edu/docview/62102717?accountid=14749

Noguera, P. A. (2008). The Trouble with Black Boys…And Other Reflections on Race, Equity, and the Future of Public Education. San Francisco, CA: Jossey-Bass

Taylor, R. W. (2010). The role of teacher education programs in creating culturally competent teachers: A moral imperative for ensuring the academic success of diverse student populations. Multicultural Education, 17(3), 24-28. Retrieved from http://libproxy.usc.edu/login?url=http://search.proquest.com.libproxy1.usc.edu/docview/815958395?accountid=14749

Walker, B. L. T. (2014). Suspended animation: A legal perspective of school discipline and African American learners in the shadows of brown. The Journal of Negro Education, 83(3), 338-351,427. Retrieved from http://libproxy.usc.edu/login?url=http://search.proquest.com.libproxy1.usc.edu/docview/1650131369?accountid=14749

7. Is Being an Educator Right for You, or Is It Just the Right Thing to Do?

Griffin, B. W. (2002). Academic Disidentification, Race, and High School Dropouts. The High School Journal, 85(4), 71–81. Retrieved from http://www.jstor.org/stable/40364355

Milanowski, A. T., Kimball, S. M., & Odden, A. (2005). Teacher accountability measures and links to learning. In L. Stiefel, A. E. Schwartz, R. Rubenstein, & J. Zabel (Eds.), Measuring school performance and efficiency: Implications for practice and research (2005 American Education Finance Association yearbook) (pp. 137–162). New York: Taylor & Francis.

Rodgers, C. (2002). Defining reflection: Another look at John Dewey and reflective thinking. Teachers College Record, 104(4), 842–866.

Rodgers, C. (2002). Reflecting-on-the-future: A chronological consideration of reflective practice. Reflective Practice: International and Multidisciplinary Perspectives, 9(2), 177–184. doi: 10.1080/14623940802005525

Rueda, R. (2011). The 3 dimensions of improving student performance. New York, NY:

Teachers College Press.

Taylor, R. W. (2010). The role of teacher education programs in creating culturally competent teachers: A moral imperative for ensuring the academic success of diverse student populations. Multicultural Education, 17(3), 24-28. Retrieved from http://libproxy.usc.edu/login?url=http://search.proquest.com.libproxy1.usc.edu/docview/815958395?accountid=14749

HadassahsCrownPublishing.com

www.ingramcontent.com/pod-product-compliance
Lightning Source LLC
Chambersburg PA
CBHW081747100526
44592CB00015B/2333